Peter Smithson: Conversations with Students

Published by
Princeton Architectural Press
37 East Seventh Street
New York, New York 10003

For a free catalog of books, call 1.800.722.6657.
Visit our web site at www.papress.com.

Published simultaneously by Editorial Gustavo Gili

For Princeton Architectural Press:
Project coordinator: Mark Lamster
Project editor: Scott Tennent

Special thanks to: Nettie Aljian, Dorothy Ball, Nicola Bednarek, Janet Behning, Megan
Carey, Penny (Yuen Pik) Chu, Russell Fernandez, Jan Haux, Clare Jacobson, John King,
Nancy Eklund Later, Linda Lee, Katharine Myers, Lauren Nelson, Molly Rouzie, Jane
Sheinman, Jennifer Thompson, Paul Wagner, Joseph Weston, and Deb Wood of Princeton
Architectural Press —Kevin C. Lippert, publisher

Peter Smithson: Conversations with Students

A Space for Our Generation

Catherine Spellman and Karl Unglaub, editors

Contents

As an Englishman who matured as an architect under the influence of a school of thought dubbed "The New Brutalism"—of which Alison and Peter Smithson were principal intellectual leaders—it is a pleasure to reflect on this prolonged conversation between Peter and the students of the College of Architecture and Environmental Design at Arizona State University, where I have been Dean for the last fifteen years. In fact, it was as a student myself, in Liverpool, that I first encountered Peter. He has mellowed somewhat over the intervening years, but the strength of his opinions is still apparent in this text.

Architecture is a cultural phenomenon, with a rich history of ideas and personalities. Each generation is conscious, and properly so, of those that preceded them. The relationships are often critical and argumentative, particularly with the immediate predecessors, but nonetheless much valued. ASU is fortunate to exist in a setting with a rich architectural history and a vital current architectural culture. Frank Lloyd Wright and Paolo Soleri still have a powerful presence in this culture. However, as a university we have the responsibility to expose our students to the broadest domains of architectural thought and action. This happens through our teaching and the teaching of a rich array of visitors, many of whom have been the teachers or colleagues of our own faculty as they matured in other places.

This conversation is an important manifestation of that process as our students explore the thinking of one of Britain's most influential architects and writers, Peter Smithson.

John Meunier

Alison and Peter Smithson, Hunstanton Secondary Modern School (1949–54), Norfolk, England. Interior of hall under construstion. Photograph, Nigel Henderson, 1954

Alison and Peter
Smithson, Cluster
City (1952–53).
Diagrammatic plan
of a small city,
Alison Smithson,
1953

Conversation 1

The following conversations are a result of several cooperations with Peter Smithson and a seminar at Arizona State University, which discussed the work and writings of Alison and Peter Smithson during the fall of 2001.

We thank Gustavo Gili, the College of Architecture and Environmental Design and the Herberger Center for Design Excellence at ASU for their support on this project. We are especially grateful to Peter Smithson for his generosity and enthusiasm for this publication and we are extremely appreciative of the students and faculty that participated in the seminar and conversations:

Luis Cruz, Nan Ellin, Sharon Haugen, Renata Hejduk, Daniel Hoffman, Victor Irizarry, Eugene Kupper, Joel Nice, Darren Petrucci, Robert Rager, Julie Russ, Max Underwood, and Stephan Willacy.

Catherine Spellman and Karl Unglaub
November 2002

Footnotes by Peter Smithson unless otherwise noted. —Eds.

In the prologue to the text Italian Thoughts[1] *you talk about generations of architects that have influenced each other—for example Filippo Brunelleschi, Leon Battista Alberti, and Francesco di Giorgio,[2] or Mies,[3] Eames,[4] and the Smithsons. How did the idea to draw these family trees develop, and what influence did they have upon your work?*

I suppose it is to do with my being from Britain. Europe is a small place, and these close relationships are formed. When I was thirty the first generation of architects that one looked to was Le Corbusier;[5] the second was Jean Prouvé[6] and Josép-Lluis Sert;[7] next were [George] Candilis, [Shadrach] Woods, and [Alexis] Josic,[8] who worked with Le Corbusier. These were the people you were talking about, and the connections between them were observable. Even though between the three generations there wasn't any copying in a stylistic sense, there was a kind of moral overlap. That's the curiosity. There's not a hint stylistically in their work, but there is a [moral] position.

Later, when Enric Miralles and Carme Pinós[9] were working, you could observe the generational influence again. I always regarded them within this lineage. But by their time, Mies and Corb had died, so what was inherited was an attitude and not a style. It was continuing.

1 Alison and Peter Smithson, "Three Generations," *Italian Thoughts* (Sweden:privately published,1993). *—Eds.*
2 "The three founding generations of Renaissance architecture were: Filippo Brunelleschi (1377–1446), Leon Battista Alberti (1404–1472), and Francesco di Giorgio (1439–1502). Through these three men ran the mainstream of the Renaissance, a span of three generations for the invention and the spread into ordinary use of a language whose intentions were wholly new." Alison and Peter Smithson, "Three Generations," 9.
3 Mies van der Rohe (1886–1969). "A building today is interesting only if it is more than itself; if it charges the space around it with connective possibilities—especially if it does this by a quietness, that up to now our sensibilities have not recognized as architecture at all, let alone seen clearly enough to isolate its characteristics— to see that it presents us with the new, softly

smiling face of our discipline." Alison and Peter Smithson, *The Heroic Period of Modern Architecture* (New York: Rizzoli International Publications, 1981), 13.
4 "In the 1950s the whole design climate was permanently changed by the work of Charles (1907–1978) and Ray Eames (1912–1988). By a few chairs and a house. Now chairs have always been the forward-runners of design change." Alison and Peter Smithson, *Changing the Art of Inhabitation* (London: Artemis London Ltd., 1994), 72.
5 "Le Corbusier (1887–1965) is a great visionary, and this word to me has a special significance, carrying a more religious meaning than words like idealist or revolutionary. For a visionary can make other people's minds take alight almost as by product of his personal struggles." Alison and Peter Smithson, *The Heroic Period of Modern Architecture*, 26.
6 "Seeing the work of Jean Prouvé (1901–1984)

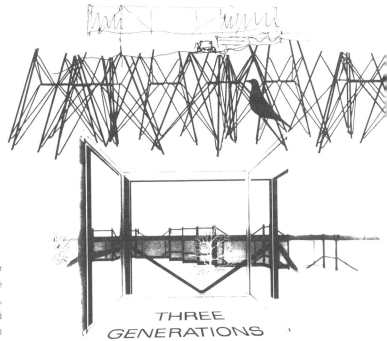

THREE
GENERATIONS

Alison and Peter Smithson,"Three Generations." Image, Lorenzo Wong and Alison Smithson, 1980

collected-up in all its astonishing fecundity for the Centre du Pompidou exhibition... one striking and totally unexpected thought: the inventiveness, the generosity of ideas is centred within the work itself; seen in its context each work or fragment seems neither to irradiate with its energy the rest of the building, nor to enrich the context. Prouvé buildings are ungenerous, seem to isolate themselves from their surroundings, sit uncomfortably, be not capable of joining." Alison and Peter Smithson, *Italienishe Gedanken, weitergedacht* (Basel: Birkhäuser, 2001), 86.

7 Josép-Lluis Sert (1902–1983) was born in Barcelona. He was of the second generation of modern architects. He worked for Le Corbusier and Prouvé in 1929 and 1930, and was later President of the Congrés Iternational d'Architecture Modern (CIAM) and dean at Harvard University's Graduate School of Design. He was the architect, inter alia, of Harvard's Peabody Terrace.

8 George Candilis (1913–1995) was born in Bakou, Russia. He had a scholarship in Paris and worked for Le Corbusier until 1950. Through Atbat-Afrique he built the Nid d'Abeilles housing in Morocco with Shadrach Woods. This project, in our view, established the base of Team 10. Later, in metropolitan France, the plan of Toulouse-Le-Mirail echoed that of our Cluster City.
Shadrach Woods (1923–1973) was born in Yonkers, New York. He had a scholarship to Dublin after serving in World War II. He was not trained as an architect, but he worked for Le Corbusier as project manager with Candilis on the Unité d'Habitation in Marseilles. Peter always thought that whatever he wrote would be under-stood by Woods, if nobody else (Alison excepted).

9 Enric Miralles (1955–2000) and Carme Pinós (1954) were with Peter in Urbino at the International Laboratory for Architecture and Urban Design in 1977 and from then on they were, all four, close.

Who did you identify with?

The second generation was very curious to us. Charles Eames, for example, was born in 1907 and therefore fell into the slot with Sert and Prouvé. He was a "joiner," so to speak—a person from North America who suddenly appeared. He went to architecture school, but he wasn't an architect. He didn't think like an architect. Nevertheless, Eames's input into the generation game was very strong, and again there is no quotation. What we are talking about is an inheritance.

Inheritance is an obsession. For example, when Mies van der Rohe first came to the United States he had an exhibition in the Museum of Modern Art,[10] which included the one building that he had completed in North America at the Illinois Institute of Technology[11] and the other building from Europe.[12] What was unknown to me until quite recently was that Eames photographed this exhibition,[13] which was the trigger, in my view, that made him change the design of his own house from a bridge-like design to the house on the ground. This was the beginning of an American link. Eames was an inheritor of a notion.

It's a game in a way, like a children's party game: identifying the moods that people like. But essentially it is ideological, insofar as the intention of our thought was not to be eclectic. This intention, of course, has

10 Mies van der Rohe, the Museum of Modern Art, New York, 1947
11 Metal and Minerals Research Building, Illinois Institute of Technology, 1942–43. This building was the source for the Royal Academy project of Peter Smithson and subsequently for the Hunstanton School. For Peter it is Mies's chef d'oeuvre in the United States. It is his "raw" building (maybe the foundation of Brutalism).
12 Haus Lange, Krefeld, Germany, 1927–30. *—Eds*.
13 The photographs appeared in *Arts and Architecture* 64, no. 27 (December 1947): 24–27. *—Eds*.

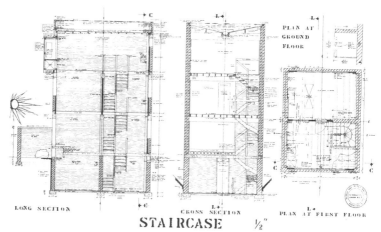

Alison and Peter Smithson, Colville Place (1952, unbuilt), London, England. Working drawing sections and plan, first-floor level, Alison and Peter Smithson, 1952

always divided North America from Europe, as every second person that emigrated to America brought with them what they had in Europe, and they "walked the walk." (I got that expression from your magazines.) For example, Thomas Jefferson[14] did fantastically well with imported architectural ideas. I always thought this was sinful, especially since in the other part of his life he was not eclectic at all.

14 Alison and Peter Smithson felt that Jefferson and Frederick Law Olmsted were the only noteworthy architects to come from America. See *Italienishe Gedanken, weitergedacht*, 70.

How important is history to the development of your work?

When I was in architecture school, I didn't go to history lectures because I thought—and this idea came from looking at one of the few modern architecture books that the school library had, a translation of [Walter] Gropius's *The New Architecture and the Bauhaus*[15]—the modern movement was always white with beautiful trees and that it didn't need history. Besides, it was always possible to get through the examination by reading up the previous two days.

I really am obsessed with history. I know a lot about Greek classicism until the end of Rome, which is when Rome moved to the Orient.[16] But I can't really mesh this knowledge of classicism with Gothic.[17] I can't retain it. I have no English, French, or German cathedrals in memory; my ability to observe the Gothic is only about the plan.

My knowledge of classicism has been built in my head exactly as the nineteenth-century architects built a memory of Gothic: I started off traveling with a list of things I had to see. When Gothic Revival[18] began, those architects did it the same way: they traveled with lists of what they knew they had to see.

15 P. Morton Shand, trans. (Cambridge, Mass.: MIT Press, 1965).
16 Fourth century. *—Eds.*
17 "Past skills are inaccessible. Because the machines, the mind, and the hand have changed; they have lost the techniques, the sensibilities and the skills they once had, and gained others. Especially inaccessable is Gothic. The Gothic mind is of course not recoverable: ordering meant something different... a different 'logic.'" Alison and Peter Smithson, *Italienishe Gedanken, weitergedacht*, 44.
18 Late eighteenth–early nineteenth century. *—Eds.*

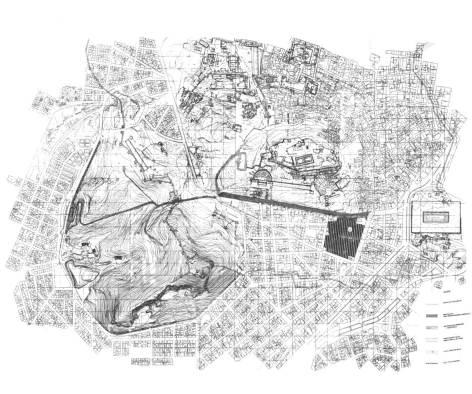

Alison and Peter
Smithson, Acropolis
Place, Athens, Greece
(1990). Plan of Athens
Archaeological Park,
Alison Smithson and
Antonio Medina
Mercendes, 1990

What was your initial list?

You see, the fact is that poor people didn't travel. Therefore, when I was fourteen or fifteen I had never been outside of England. The first places I went to were India and Burma because of World War II. My first experience of architecture outside my own country was the Hindu temples and a Buddhist monastery. I visited only one because during the war there was other work to do. These places were shattering to me. The Christian medieval monasteries were usually segregated, but in Burma you saw men, women, and children together. The youngest children wore pale lemon yellow silk and the elders wore dark brown; in between where all shades across that spectrum. (During its original exhibition, the Eiffel Tower was painted in this color range, dark brown at the bottom and yellow at the top. Now it's just a sort of gray lump.)

When the war was over, I made an effort to look at buildings in my own country, especially in Cambridge. Then, as a student, I went to Scandinavia and Alison went to Paris, and that experience really stayed with her. The first well-known modern architect I met was Arne Jacobsen.[19] My point is that at first you find yourself in places that you never expected to be in, but it is not as random as it sounds. Between 1939 and 1949 there was no new architecture in Europe; building ceased because of the war. To see a new building that had been built during those ten years, you had to go to Scandinavia[20] or South America. The whole Brazilian thing[21] occurred during the wartime period, but it was so far away.

---

19 Arne Jacobsen (1902–1971) spent the war in Sweden because he was Jewish. He was wonderfully hospitable to two students (R. T. Simpson and myself) in a house of his design.
20 "Scandinavia was where most architects qualifying immediately before the war—and after— looked for models of what to build... for there was a socialist democratic society that had built for all its needs." Alison and Peter Smithson, *Italienishe Gedanken, weitergedacht*, 10.
21 Brazil decided to move its capital from Rio de Janeiro to a central location in order to encourage the development of the country. Brazil became a Republic in 1881, and the new constitution stated that the government would allocate 14,000 square kilometers in the center of Brazil for the construction of the new capital. It was not until 1956, however, that the capital of Brazil, which was regarded as a Utopian City, was constructed. Lucio Costa designed the master plan while Oscar Niemeyer designed the buildings. See David Epstein, *Brasília: Plan and Reality* (Berkeley: University of California Press, 1973). –Eds.

What I was looking at while traveling was also partly about seeing what building was like—not architecture, but what construction was like. My other pursuit was to get to know one's own place—the cathedrals, etc. Then I went to the Royal Academy Schools in London for a year because the professor was good in the study of classicism. I thought if one was an enemy of eclecticism, then one had to know more about it than they did. In a sense this was a wartime idea—the general of one side had a picture of the general on the other side in his caravan; he wanted to know as much as possible of the history of his opponent. So that was what I was doing: trying to find out how the other side thinks.

My later obsession, together with Alison, was to know all the buildings of Le Corbusier and later all the buildings of Mies van der Rohe, but not to copy them. It was like being a priest who follows the journeys of the evangelical saints, traveling from place to place. A modern priest says, "I must make that journey." It's an obsession. He is engaging that movement into himself. I'm sorry if it sounds romantic—it is romantic.

Hunstanton Secondary Modern School. Perspective, Peter Smithson, 1950

Do you have a classical leaning?

During a conversation I recently had in Paris with Axel Sowa[22] about classicism, out of the blue I suddenly thought about Andy Warhol and his multiple repetitions. Warhol used a classical conversational method. Sowa was explaining how classicism is recycled into our period, and it dawned on me that you examine classicism as modes of operation, rather than as images you can see. For me, classicism is central to my thought. It is a result of ten years or so of looking at all the Le Corbusier structures and another ten years looking at Mies van der Rohe buildings and then ten or fifteen years of looking at all the Doric temples and classical Greek towns.[23] I make it sound very serious, but in fact that was how we spent our holidays!

Before the war, the art historian Rudolf Wittkower came to England to continue his research of classical art and architecture. After forty or so years (I exaggerate), he wrote a book, which represented this very long period of study, and it is one interpretation of classicism.[24] Vincent Scully also wrote a book about Greek temples after a relatively short period of study—five years or so—and it presents another interpretation of classicism, because it had been interpreted romantically.[25]

22 Axel Sowa is an editor of *L'Architecture d'Aujourdhui*. –Eds.

23 We studied Doric Temples from early (the Argive Heraeum) to late (Nemea); we also studied Greek towns—Athens being the only one with substantial above-ground "remains." Our principle essays on classicism are "Space and Greek Architecture," in *The Listener* (October 1958) and "Theories Concerning the Layout of Classical Greek Buildings," in *AA Journal* (February 1959).

24 *The Architectural Principles in the Age of Humanism* (New York: W. W. Norton, 1971).

25 *The Earth, the Temple and the Gods* (New Haven: Yale University Press, 1979). Scully's book is much more subjective. We really do not know how the Ancient Greeks thought or how such perfection was reached.

Were you acquainted with Colin Rowe and his interpretations of classicism?

I knew Colin Rowe, but I've never read any of his writings. He was, in a way, my enemy [laughing]. But with all of these people of a similar age group, enmity is a very complicated issue. He was of the circle of Wittkower, and you could say that through this circle we became engaged with art history.

In the beginning of our conversation in Paris, Axel Sowa was thinking, "In what way is classicism represented in our period?" Then I made a kind of sudden jump into repetition. I thought back to a trip to Spain when I visited a gallery in Madrid. There is one painting by Gentile Bellini of an annunciation with an angel and Mary, and it has a line going up the street and then a flat building at the end.[26] It is from the thirteenth or fourteenth century and has a landscape in the background. It is sort of a "pre-classical classicism"—classicism without guile. Thinking about it you suddenly wonder, "why am I so interested? Why do I go back to a gallery to see one picture?" In Montreal, in Mies's Westmount Centre,[27] you look through the architecture to the landscape beyond—it's a classical device.

26 *La Annunciación*, Gentile Bellini (1429–1507), 1465. The building which terminates the line is a fictional structure.
27 A late distinguished, if academic, work in a city rather short of such things.

How did you start interpreting the ancient Greek and Italian cities?

One of the observations that Alison and I made in Greece was whether, in the formulation of the defensive walls, there was any relationship between the wall geometry and the street geometry.[28]

What do you think started the shift from nineteenth-century revivalism to the modern movement?

I believe the modern movement[29] began with the language of cubism.[30] The three subsequent generations were not so indebted to cubism. It all began before World War I—that is, with cubism in France, with constructivism in Russia, and with futurism in Italy.[31] In 1910 and 1913 architecture jumped off, in my view, from painting.

28 Only in Palmanova, a defensive city outside of Venice from the post-Vauban period, does this relationship exist.
29 "What was the first modern building? This is commonly supposed to be a meaningless question, but if we accept that something did happen round about the first world war, that a new way of thinking, which was manifest in the new style, came into being, then there must be some building in which this new style was first apparent. Essentially, a 'Modern Architecture' was: Cubic, or appeared to be carved out of cubes geometrically organized and highly abstract in its interpretation of human activities, a complete thing in itself. It was poised, not rooted to its site. It was usually white or brightly coloured, or made of shiny materials. Natural materials, when used, appear to be substitutes for artificial materials not yet invented." Alison and Peter Smithson, *The Heroic Period of Modern Architecture*, 9.
30 Modern Architecture begins in 1922, for that is the date of Le Corbusier's villa at Vaucresson and of Oud's Café de Unie in Rotterdam. Then begin the new forms in architecture, forms from painting; Le Corbusier's forms may be the child of a single painting, one more or less completely flat and heavily indebted to the rectangle of the

Alison and Peter Smithson with Nigel Henderson, Eduardo Paolozzi, and Roland Jenkins, Parallel of Life and Art exhibition (1953). Photograph, Nigel Henderson, 1953

frame: Picasso's *Bottle of Vieur Marc, Glass, Guitar and Newspaper*, 1913. From this Le Corbusier's villas grow: Garches (1927) and Poissy (1929–31). It was a long gestation.
31. Cubism is an early 20th-century school of painting in which realistic detail is eliminated in favor of geometric forms portraying subject matter in pure abstraction. See Neil Cox, *Cubism* (London: Phaidon Press, 2000).
Constructivism is an abstract art movement that emerged in Europe in the 1920s. It was invented by the Russian avant garde in the 1910s and was first transplanted to the Bauhaus in Germany by such figures as Vladimir Tatlin and Wassily Kandinsky. See Sima Ingberman, *ABC International Constructivist Architecture, 1922–1939* (Cambridge, Mass.: MIT Press, 1994). Futurism was a brief utopian phase of early modernism when artists felt on the verge of a new age. They took a violent departure from traditional forms so as to express movement and growth. See Marjorie Perloff, *The Futurist Movement: Avant-garde, Avant Guerre and the Language of Rupture* (Chicago: University of Chicago Press, 1986), 115. *—Eds.*

In the **Team 10 Primer,**[32] *there is a great feeling of opportunity, revolutionary thought, and generosity between the generations involved. How would you advise the younger generation of architects today to move forward in a similar fashion?*

In the modern era, there wasn't any confrontation. What's difficult to understand is that the generations remained the strongest of friends, to death. [Siegfried] Giedion[33] and Le Corbusier were both extremely kind to the younger generation. I suppose they were just extreme heroes. Le Corbusier said at the time that the people who are forty are the people who have the energy. When you are sixty or seventy you start to lose both the revolutionary fervor and the energy to crystallize a project so that it becomes not only a project but also a demonstration and an ideology.

---

32 "The object of this *Primer* is to put into one document those articles, essays, and diagrams which Team 10 regard as being central to their individual positions. In a way it is a history of how the ideas of the people involved have grown and changed as a result of contact with the others, and it is hoped that the publication of these root ideas, in their original often naïve form, will enable them to continue life. . . .
"They came together in the first place, certainly because of mutual realization of the inadequacies of the processes of architectural thought which they had inherited from the modern movement as a whole, but more important, each sensed that

the other had found some way towards a new beginning. This new beginning, and the long build-up that followed, has been concerned with inducing, as it were, into the bloodstream of the architect an understanding and feeling for the patterns, the aspirations, the artifacts, the tools, the modes of transportation and communications of present-day society, so that he can as a natural thing build towards that society's realization-of-itself." Alison Smithson, ed. *Team 10 Primer* (Cambridge, Mass.: MIT Press, 1968), 2–3.
33 Siegfried Giedion (1888–1968) was a professional art historian and secretary of CIAM.

How was the transition from the CIAM to Team 10 made?

I think that is in the documentation.[34] Keep in mind when you are dealing with only one person's recollection, there is only a single viewpoint. That recollection is not history, in the sense that history is a man collecting information and then saying, "now, it looks as if such and such happened." With recollection, there's only one witness. Every year there are five books on Napoleon, and he's been dead 200 years. Even the facts can be interpreted by a single person differently.

CIAM was organized in national groups. At the Dubrovnik meeting,[35] we agreed that each person who represented his or her national group would agree to destroy it, so that another team could be started. This was also mixed up with language. CIAM was a French organization and its documentation was all in French. In the wartime/postwar period, western allies precipitated English as the international language, which meant architecture and art centered around Paris in the late 1940s faded. We were also engaged in changing intellectual disputes into English. Yet somehow the French were antagonistic to Americans— very strange.

On very practical terms, England had a harder time rebuilding after the war than Germany, even though England had more Marshall Plan aid per capita than they did. Germany succeeded by hard work. The Americanization of Germany really wasn't visible until the end of the 1950s.

His "feel" for Le Corbusier's work—a fellow
Swiss—was a lifelong devotion.
34 The transition from CIAM to Team 10 is well
recorded. See Alison Smithson, "Team 10 out of
CIAM," *Team 10 Primer*, 3–24.
35 CIAM 10, held in Dubrovnik, Yugoslavia, was
the meeting from which the name Team 10 arose.

Have your ideas about architecture changed over the years?

I think only very little. Recently I saw a traveling exhibition in Zürich called As Found,[36] which deals with architecture, photography, theater, and cinema in the 1950s. Later, at a meeting of the AA [Architectural Association, London]—because one of the sponsors of the exhibition was there—I said two or three things referring to the exhibit, one of which was the aphorism of Mies van der Rohe: architecture begins when you bring three bricks carefully together, while Brutalism[37] begins when you are trying to uncover the brick-ness of brick. It is very much a physical thing, about the quality. Certainly Mies was very concerned with the geometric quality, with his background as a marble mason. But his building was slightly different—more metaphysical.

I showed one slide at that meeting of the backyard of an old house with a brick wall and a tree, which was left within the building. This slide was trying to show the tree-ness of the tree and the brick-ness of the brick. And correctly, I think, it had probably been interpreted as very much like Japanese traditional architecture—we had books of Japanese architecture.[38] Because there was a German architect [Bruno Taut] who worked in Japan in the 1930s, Japanese traditional architecture was transmitted into Europe.

The other thing is the issue of time. Why did I do something fifty years ago? You can disbelieve anything I remember about fifty years ago, because it is over the edge of real memory.

36 As Found: The Independent Group and The Brutalist Movement in England During the Fifties, at Museum für Gestaltung Zürich, Switzerland, March 3, 2001–June 13, 2001. —Eds.
37 "Through Japanese architecture, the longings of the generation of Garnier and Behrens found form... producing in Le Corbusier the purist aesthetic of the sliding screens, continuous space, the power of white and earth colors on the rendered wall... in Mies, the structure and the screen as absolutes. Our understanding—and so it might have been for Mies—was that for the Japanese their Form was only part of a general conception of life, a sort of reverence for the

natural world and from that, for the materials of the built world. It is this respect for materials, a realization of the affinity which can be established between building and man—which was at the root of our way of seeing and thinking about things that we called New Brutalism." Alison and Peter Smithson, Without Rhetoric: An Architectural Aesthetic 1955–1972 (London: Latimer New Dimensions Limited, 1973), 6. Our understanding of Brutalism had little to do with the Brutalism that popularly became lumped into the style outlined in Reyner Banham's The New Brutalism, (New York: Reinhold, 1966).
38 For instance, Jiro Harada, The Lesson of

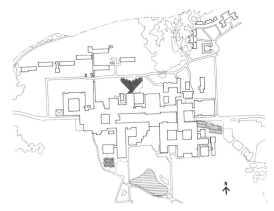

Alison and Peter Smithson, extensions of University of Bath, England (1978–88). Site plan, Alison and Peter Smithson and Lorenzo Wong, 1989

"This room looks like where you would sell refrigerators"[39]—I think that's marvelous. It causes you to think, doesn't it? What is the room like where we talk, where we exchange ideas? This room could be anywhere.

Your early work with the Independent Group[40] focuses on the relationship between life and art. What do you think about this now?

I speak about this idea in the lecture.[41] But certainly the work that was done in Bath in the 1980s,[42] which is very disliked, is an attempt, in a more complex way, to connect the lives of the people, the life of the services, and the life of the fabric together, which results in what is interpreted by outsiders as slightly sloppy architecture.

Japanese Architecture (The Studio Ltd., 1936).
39 A remark of Giancarlo De Carlo's in Venice.
40 The Independent Group at the Institute of Arts in London was a private association of artists, architects, historians, and critics who met intermittently between 1952 and 1955 to discuss questions of aesthetics and interchange between the artistic disciplines. They supported ideas that promoted mass culture and challenged elitist hierarchies within society. See David Robins, ed., *The Independent Group: Postwar Britain and the Aesthetics of Plenty* (Cambridge, Mass.: MIT Press, 1990), 8. —*Eds.*

41 See *The Response to the Glut* in this book, 52–69. —*Eds.*
42 The Smithsons built a number of buildings at the University of Bath: Amenity Building (1978–80, 1984–85); Animal House (1981); Arts Barn (1980–81, 1990); School of Architecture and Engineering Building (1982–88); Porch to University Hall (1983); and Second Arts Building (1979–81). —*Eds.*

Can you discuss your ideas about consumer culture[43] **and explain how they are related to the development of the media, television, and advertising?**

Yes, and this is why the lecture is called *The Response to the Glut*. Glut means "too much." What position do you take with the "too much"? What the lecture deals with is the notion of controlling the "too much" so that you can be in the room. On television, you can see a lady talking and behind her there are twenty-five screens, each screen with different information. That information has nothing to do with what she is saying. They are out to confuse you—not to allow you to have your own thoughts. The television is there to sell the product. Even the news is paid for by somebody. On the television this morning was an interview about dogs. They had a man and a woman, and then there were fifty other people, also talking, and then twelve puppies in the middle. It was absolutely loaded with information. You can't consume it. Back in America's Revolutionary time, what the lawyers were saying was much too complicated for the people at large to understand—the rights of man, that whole intellectual thing. Maybe I'm being childish, thinking that, but it has an innocent charm; writing rules was for the purification of the culture. Architecture is not in that game.

But architecture is kind of a puritan thing. What springs to my mind is the Hochschule für Gestaltung in Ulm by Max Bill, which I think is the best building in Germany in the twentieth century.[44] It creates

43 "When Le Corbusier assembled *Vers Une Architecture*, he gave to young architects everywhere a way of looking at the emergent machine-served society, and from that, a way of looking at antiquity and a rationale to support his personal aesthetic. Viollet-le-Duc had performed the same service to architects before Le Corbusier: the role they played is traditional to the development of architecture.... [W]e try to do the same as these architects before us. We write to make ourselves see what we have got in the inescapable present... to give another interpretation of the same ruins... to show a glimpse of another aesthetic. The real

implications were hidden from us when we started thinking out our position and response to the advertisements contained in the glossy magazines of the fifties. Our interest and fascination were a seeming anachronism to our New Brutalist stance unless you read the advertisement images as visual telegrams with a specially loaded message about possibilities for the immediate future." Alison and Peter Smithson, *Without Rhetoric*, 1.
44 Max Bill (1908–1994) is of the second generation. The Hochschule is one of the few generating buildings of the twentieth century.

something very important on a hillside without any rhetoric at all.
People take positions about the Hochschule für Gestaltung. That seems
to be a marvelous thing to me. I don't believe it myself that this is
the work of Max Bill. He does not design like that. An assistant, in my
view, developed the building. The thing the Eameses contributed to
architecture is the acceptance of the collaborative opposite side, which
is that someone could do a piece of a project, and it could completely
change the direction of the project. I'm wondering whether there
was someone in Max Bill's office who had different feelings about
architecture than Bill had. I am describing the kind of spaces in which
emptiness plays a part.

You wrote an essay called the "Aesthetics of Change." [45] ***Do you think of modern society today as transient and nomadic?***

What we were talking about at the time was a language of what is fixed and what is transient. It was saying—which turns out to be fairly true—that because it is such a big investment, the urban motorway system tends to be fixed, but housing developments tend to be reflective and tend to be affected by change. But the paradox, having just come back from Paris, is that the buildings have remained unchanged in my lifetime and in Hemingway's lifetime; there is a romanticism about Paris that it is unchanging. Therefore, what remains fixed and what is changed is a very complicated thing. Even the Eames's house was changing, in terms of the relationship of the bluff to the sea, etc.

45 "The object . . . was to define the aesthetics of change; the form systems that follow naturally from the ideas of Mobility, Cluster, and so on. . . .
"To find a built example of the new aesthetic we have to look at the Eames House in Santa Monica, California. Built in 1949 its apparent casualness implies 'change,' a message carried both by its aesthetic, and by its genuine lightness.
"This building's aesthetic of expendability is quite outside the European tradition, but if we need transient buildings we must face up to creating a transient aesthetic." Alison and Peter Smithson, *Ordinariness and Light* (Cambridge, Mass.: MIT Press, 1970), 154–59.

How would you describe your collaboration with Alison?

It was friendly enmity. We were very reciprocal, each the other half. Her talents and my talents were completely different. I think it's a normal thing with partnerships. Even the family side was not alike, but reciprocal. The books with Monacelli Press[46] are an example of this reciprocity. It is not like the Eames's book,[47] where the complete list of their assistants is running along the top of the page for each job. We don't have a record like that, but every drawing is attributed, and it says whether Alison or I was the lead architect. On a big project we would both work on it, yet someone was making the major contribution; somebody invented the format and became the lead. It is not a conscious act—as you are developing a project, someone takes the lead.

46 Alison and Peter Smithson, *The Charged Void: Architecture* (New York: Monacelli Press, 2001) and *The Charged Void: Urbanism* (New York: Monacelli Press, 2004). —*Eds*.
47 John Neuhart and Marilyn Neuhart, contributor Ray Eames, *Eames Design: The Work of the Office of Charles and Ray Eames* (New York : H. N. Abrams, 1989). —*Eds*.

Alison and Peter
Smithson, Yellow
Lookout (1991),
Tecta, Lauenförde.
Photograph, Peter
Smithson, 1995

Reflecting on your life as an architect, what is your major frustration concerning the profession?

Long periods without work, but of course that's why we entered so many competitions. In the 1980s, we were building a series of buildings for the University of Bath. In the 1990s we were building a series of projects for Axel Bruchhäuser in Germany.[48] In that ten-year period in the 1960s, we might have entered fifteen or twenty competitions. If you don't have work, then you have to learn to live without money.

48 The Toilet Tree (1986–90); Tecta Paths (1990);
Tecta Canteen Porch (1990); Yellow Lookout
(1991); Riverbank Window, Hexenhaus (1990);
Hexenhaus Holes (1990); Hexenbesenraum,
Hexenhaus (1990–96); Tecta Yard Gates (1992);
Axel's Office Porch (1995); Tecta Signage (1995);
The Meadow (1996); The Mill Porch (1996–97);
Panorama Porch (1997–98); Metal Workshop
Porch (1998–2000); and Father's Room (1999).
—*Eds.*

Was that an opportunity for you to work on your writing during that time?

That's when you work. I always say it takes twenty years from the notion of a building to its realization. Before the construction of the Economist Building [1959–64], we were studying Mies's tall buildings in Chicago. Originally, the aluminum was not anodized; therefore, the windows after ten to fifteen years became covered with a white material. Therefore, 860 Lakeshore Drive was later painted with grey paint.

In the ten years before 1959, I was looking at metal buildings in the United States to see how they behaved. At that time Chicago had quite high pollution, as did New York. I knew that these materials would be changed by that pollution.

Alison once said to Lou Kahn [49] "What did you do in the 1930s, Lou?" and he said, "I lived in a city called Le Corbusier!" What a fantastic reply. Without work, you're living a life of investigation and pleasure of other people's effort.

49 Lou Kahn (1901–1974) seemed to us in the
1960s a displaced European architect.

Alison and Peter Smithson,
St. Hilda's College, Oxford
(1967–70), Oxford, England.
Photograph from garden side,
Peter Smithson, 1971

Conversation 2

Footnotes by Peter Smithson unless otherwise noted. *–Eds.*

Can you summarize which events of each decade had the biggest effect on you?

The biggest individual impact was the decade of the 1960s, when the Berlin Free University was designed.[1] It was a real mat-building,[2] which invented a new building type in that it combined the skills of Jean Prouvé from the end of the 1930s and the development of Josic, Candillis, and Woods. I thought that was the most important building of our period—that is, the last half of the twentieth century—because it isn't very often that a new building type is evolved. In the nineteenth century there was the railway station, for which there had been no precedent.

What we were talking about yesterday as we were walking down the street, was, "does one build a network in a city like Phoenix?" Here at the Arches [Plaza],[3] with its plants overhead and the overhead shade, you are utilizing a new model, but in fact it is a reinvention of the Arabic town plan, with its narrow, self-shading streets.

I think it is a very difficult question—what you recall in each decade. In one's own life, often things happen at the same time. The House of the Future occurred the same year as the creation of Team 10 and the Sugden House. The events overlap. I said that usually a building takes twenty years from invention to realization, which is true. However, the first stage of the Berlin Free University was finished in 1973, the competition design was from 1963, and most of the Prouvé ideas were formed in the 1930s.[4]

1 The university was designed by Candilis, Josic, Woods, and Schiedhelm in 1964. —Eds.
2 "Mat-buildings can be said to epitomize the anonymous collective; where the function comes to enrich the fabric, and the individual gains new freedoms of action through a new shuffled order, based on interconnection, close-knit patterns of association, and possibilities for growth, diminution, and change." Alison Smithson, "How to Recognise and Read Mat-Buildings," in Hashim Sarkis, et al, ed. Le Corbusier's Venice Hospital (Munich: Prestel, 2001), 91.
3 The Arches Plaza, 112 University Dr., Tempe, AZ. Peter and students were talking about the network of in-between spaces in downtown Tempe on the first day of his visit. —Eds.
4 Prouvé's ideas about facades with folded metal were applied at the Market in Clichy in 1939.

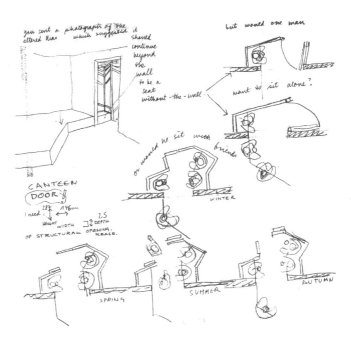

Alison Smithson,
Canteen Porch (1990),
Tecta, Lauenförde.
Exploratory sketches,
Alison Smithson

When you and Alison would begin a project, what would you start with?

I always start in a very banal way when I have a given program: with the room sizes. I would draw out the whole program to a scale that I'm going to then design with, in order to get a fixed volume to manipulate.[5]

5 "Looking back it would seem that almost from the beginning, certainly since 1952, there has been conscious persistence along the following lines... the seeing of, the study of, and the working with towns and cities as fabrics, the importance of the idea of the street and the ordering of buildings through their internal ways, and lastly... there is in almost every work some part—a court or yard, a walk or garden—which cannot be touched by later building activity." Alison and Peter Smithson, "Set of Mind," *Italian Thoughts*, 100.

What role does play have in your work?

It is never a conscious thing, the use of play. I noticed between my children and my grandchildren the aspect of play is far more prevalent than it ever was between me and my children. Maybe that is the case with all parents; children are just nice animals that we have about. But there is also the sensation that I'm sure every parent experiences in a way: you relive part of your life through your children, particularly the school and college years. You re-remember what you were like. (I was very happy as a student. No responsibilities. Stupid teachers.)

I think play doesn't have the same role for us as it did in the sense that Charles Eames used the concept of play. For us it was the joke. Maybe it is an English thing—verbal jokes, misusing words. Eames had that as well.

6 "The studies of association and identity led to the development of systems of linked building complexes which were intended to correspond more closely to the network of social relationships, as they now exist, than the existing patterns of infinite spaces and self-contained buildings. These freer systems are more capable of change, and, particularly in new communities, of mutating in scale and intention as they go along.
"It was realized that the essential error of the English New Towns was that they were too rigidly conceived, and in 1956 we put forward an alternative system in which the 'infra-structure' (roads and services) was the only fixed thing. The road system was devised to be simple and to give equal ease of access to all parts.
"This theme of the road system as the basis of the community structure was further explored in the Cluster City idea between 1957 and 1959, in the Haupstadt Berlin Plan 1958, and in the London Roads Study 1959." Alison Smithson, ed., *Team 10 Primer*, 52.
7 "Instead of our towns being laid out in massive quadrangles, with the streets in narrow trenches walled in by seven-storeyed buildings set perpendicular on pavement and enclosing unhealthy courtyards, airless and sunless wells,

How important is sociology for your work?

Sociology was virtually an unknown academic discipline in England, but a strong one in France. After the war, the old universities began to have courses in anthropology that focused on our own culture. This was the start of sociology as a discipline in England. We were at the beginning of this development because our friend Judith Henderson studied anthropology as sociology at Cambridge University during this time. The development of sociology came about because working-class boys who were veterens suddenly could attend Oxford and Cambridge because they received educational funding from the state. Their social interests started this.

The shifting of an abstract notion about society to something real was the whole Team 10 business as well.[6] There were two forces in modern architecture before the Second World War: the first was the language and social intention derived from cubism and constructivism in Russia before the First World War; the second was Le Corbusier's writing about how unhygienic Paris was.[7] The classic example of this is that the greatest number of cases of tuberculosis in Europe were in Stockholm, but you would have never believed it from a culture that we associate with cleanliness, open air, and so forth. Stockholm was not like that before modern architecture and socialism; it was a culture change. So you are trying to read the social context, which is terribly difficult, because you are in it. It is much easier when you are working as an outsider, like an anthropologist. When we worked in Kuwait,[8] we were reading it as outsiders. We were not in it, we were observing it.

our layout, employing the same area and housing the same number of people, would show great blocks of houses with successive setbacks, stretching along arterial avenues." Le Corbusier, *Towards a New Architecture* (London: Architectural Press, 1927), 59. —*Eds.*
8 Alison and Peter Smithson, Kuwait Mat-Building, (1969–70). "The architectural language of the demonstration mat-building is one of protection." Alison and Peter Smithson, *The Charged Void: Architecture*, 356.

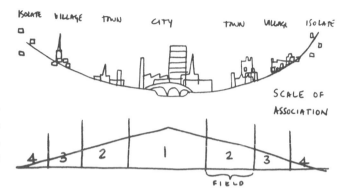

Alison and Peter
Smithson, Doorn
Manifesto (1954).
Diagram

How important are the diagrams to the development of your work?

Very little. Somebody recently asked why we used the diagram that Patrick Geddes got from [Frédérick] Le Play about the relationship of the communities to the topography.[9] That is, in the valleys were the big cities and higher up were the separate farms. This person was asking how that came to us, and I said it was because there had been a Patrick Geddes revival after the war and that we had it from our teachers. You could say that was a gift, a kind of recycled gift. Patrick Geddes's input into urbanism disappeared, like you could say [Charles Rennie] Mackintosh's input diminished.[10] Mackintosh didn't die until 1928, but from 1910 until his death, he was forgotten. Now you can buy a Mackintosh ashtray. There's a cycle.

9 Patrick Geddes (1854–1932), working from the
French sociologist Frédérick Le Play's
(1806–1882) *Place, Work and Folk* (London:
Longmans, 1970).
10 Charles Rennie Mackintosh's (1868–1928)
Hill House in Helensburgh is a masterpiece.

I think you can take credit for introducing the diagram as something more than just what it had been up until that point. It had a sort of allegorical significance for Le Corbusier and for Geddes and so forth. But your own diagrams, which you used to demonstrate webs and networks, were a new contribution to the discipline of architectural representation. Those are very strong logograms in our imagination, and we continue to refer back to them as being seminal to a particular way of thinking.

Yes, because there was the other side of diagrams. The [Louis] Kahn diagram, for example, where you have "stop" streets and "go" streets and parking, was a factual diagram of a possible real reorganization of the city, and a conceptual diagram at the same time.[11] The trouble with using nonfactual diagrams, like when you make a collage, is that then you need someone to read it. Diagrams have to be legible and buildable. Interestingly enough, Kahn was entirely spontaneous when making diagrams. Or so I think, because for that first building he did for the Blue Cross/Blue Shield,[12] the front door was on an eighteen-lane highway. That is, he hadn't remodeled his mind to see that you can't build an ordinary, old-fashioned bank building up against a multilane highway. This is again an example of the mind working separately, as the left and right of the brain work separately. So the answer to that is the diagram takes many forms, of which the most useful, in my view, is very close to being realistic.

11 Philadelphia Study diagrams by Louis Kahn, in
Alison Smithson, ed., *Team 10 Primer*, 53. *—Eds.*
12 Louis Kahn, AFL-CIO Medical Center,
Philadelphia (1951–1958), demolished. *—Eds.*

Alison and Peter
Smithson, Government
Offices, Kuwait (1970).
Drawing, Lorenzo Wong,
1994

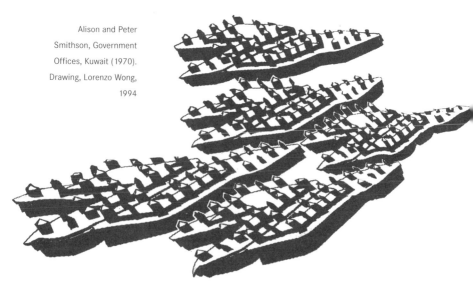

Why don't we see more models in your work?

I hate models because they get between you and visualizing the reality. I know Mies used models. I can see a certain use for models of the realistic type, like the kind of "one-is-to-one" profile of the windows, so that you have a physical example. But these types of models are made of wood and painted, and as soon as the real material is in place, your impression changes completely.

*When you and Alison collaborated with the members of
the Independent Group, what were your hopes for the
integration of art and architecture?*

This is particularly interesting to me at the moment, because there's just
been a first book about Nigel Henderson.[13] For me, the Independent
Group was like a schoolboy association. I am making it sound ridiculous,
but it was all sorts of nudging and giggling. This picks up with the earlier
questions about generations and sociology. Judith Henderson, Nigel
Henderson's wife, was originally Judith Stevens. Virginia Stevens, who
was Judith's aunt, became Virginia Woolf when she married. Of course
they are two generations apart. The Stevens family in the past were
Quakers and had notions about serving the community. Judith Henderson
was a student of sociology and anthropology at Cambridge in the
postwar period that I was talking about earlier. She was working in the
poor part of London as an observer for a sociological study. In this book
there are a lot of marvelous pictures of their little street. There is a story
about when the war-damage repairmen came, the Hendersons persuaded
them to install a bath. Theirs was the only bath on that street. It is
unimaginable to you, as Phoenix is unimaginable to me.

Nigel Henderson and Eduardo Paolozzi[14] had a spontaneous affection
for each other. That is, both exhibitions[15] we did with them were done
with a minimum of discussion because, like a love affair, there was a
confluence of understanding. For five years or longer we were very
important to each other, and then it faded. Like in the 1920s between
Braque and Picasso, there was this close friendship for a short period.
The book by Victoria Walsh gives a good explanation of this period.

13 Victoria Walsh, *Nigel Henderson* (London:
Thames and Hudson, 2001). —*Eds*.
14 Eduardo Paolozzi (1924–), a catalystic figure in
postwar art.
15 Parallel of Life and Art, Institute of
Contemporary Arts, London, 1953, and Patio and
Pavillion, as part of the This is Tomorrow
exhibition, Whitehill Chapel Art Gallery, London,
1956. —*Eds*.

Alison Smithson,
Hexenbesenraum
(1990–96),
Hexenhaus, Bad
Karlshafen,
Germany.
Axonometric, Roger
Paez di Blanc, 1996

Now that we know that natural resources are not inexhaustible, what do you think is the responsibility of the architect relative to materials?

Since 1986 we have been working in Germany for Axel Bruchhäuser at Tecta. We have always used very old building techniques and materials like bits of wood. I suppose the stainless-steel sheet is the only thing that wasn't there when I was a boy, as it were. It is all very corny.
Of course, as an architect you're tied up with the business of resources. Metal buildings, like metal aircraft, demand a tremendous amount of resources and energy to make them; and although you get minimum weight with fabric, that minimum weight costs you a lot. That's why Buckminster Fuller was a banana, if you don't mind me saying so about one of your citizens. He thought that weight condemns cathedrals because they are so heavy.[16]

16 The relic of Buckminster Fuller's (1895–1983)
Dome in Montreal is rather good.

In the House of the Future,[17] *was there an idea about using new technology and materials that were developed during the war?*

The main idea about the House of the Future was not to do with technology. It ran parallel with the Monsanto House of the Future,[18] which was just a bungalow, a bit of a plastic house in a garden. I thought that the project was corny. We said that you don't get a new house without a new urban fabric. We did a house that was inward looking, and the garden was placed inside of the house. This was a different formulation—a new piece of urbanism. It was specific—modern for couples, old people, and small children. It was not the typical family house with a garden. Most cities contain a multitude of house types. You have an enormous choice available, disregarding the money problem (there are all of these houses that you might like but can't afford). There are hundreds and hundreds of types. The idea of a new type for a new situation was not very realistic. You could say it was idealistic.

Some of the things went wildly wrong. In the 1950s, oil prices were reduced steadily every year, and suddenly they seemed low. Therefore, people like the Eameses made molded plastic chairs—it seemed reasonable. You still could not afford to build heavy things using plastic, but at the time it was reasonable to assume that if the price of oil continued to drop every year, in twenty-five years it would be reasonably cheap. Now, you would worry about using oil-based products because the price is quite high. However, when you look at the freeways here in Phoenix, you would think that nobody worries about oil. I don't understand it; it is as if the whole globe was full of oil.

17 House of the Future (1955–56) tried to project what would be in general use after twenty-five years. "The general conception of the house: The rooms flow into one another like the compartments of a cave, and as in a cave, the skewered passage which joins one compartment with another effectively maintains privacy." Alison and Peter Smithson, *The Charged Void: Architecture*, 164.

18 The *House of the Future* by the Monsanto Corporation opened in Disneyland in June 1957, made entirely of plastic. At the time of its demolition ten years later, the wrecking ball bounced off the plastic surface and the house had to be demolished by hand. *—Eds.*

Is there a relationship between the Eames house[19] and your House of the Future?

Again, it was very interesting. In exchange for writing the foreword to the Nigel Henderson book, the publisher gave me a credit for books. One of the books I chose was the Eameses' black book,[20] which I'd bought when it came out but threw away because I thought it was terrible. Later I felt I needed it, because the book starts with all the experiments with molding furniture in the 1940s. The 1948 house was possible because of the climate—it didn't need heating or double-glazing, so you can have a soft building, without solid walls or climate control. It is very specific to that location. Again, you have to explain how the house came to be developed in that way. At first the design was for a bridge house. Then Charles went to the Museum of Modern Art to photograph the Mies exhibition, at a time when Mies had only built one building in America. This exhibition changed Eames's thinking, just like in the 1930s when people went to see the Weissenhof Siedlung[21] and were changed by that experience. I think Eames was changed by seeing the nature of the first building that Mies did here in the United States, which was built with standard windows. But this is a hypothesis. I arrived at this hypothesis after Eames died, so there is no way of checking. Perhaps the steelwork came and they got a bigger volume by putting the house on the ground. Charles had this spontaneous way of working that he was so good at. But he wasn't an architect, you see, though he went to architecture school.

19 The Eames house was built in 1948, but not known to the Smithsons until much later. See Alison and Peter Smithson, "Eames Celebration," in *Architecture Design* 36 (September 1966): 432–71.
20 John Neuhart and Marilyn Neuhart, contributor Ray Eames, *Eames Design. —Eds*.
21 Weissenhof Siedlung, Stuttgart, Germany, the catalystic housing "exhibition," in 1927.

Breakfast with Ray
at the Eames house.
Photograh, Peter
Smithson, 1978

Where did you meet Charles Eames?

In 1957 or 1958 you couldn't get money to travel. I went to Chicago
through an invitation from Peter Carter,[22] who took care of me there. Then
Charles did something unbelievable: he sent the money for a ticket on
the California Zephyr for me to go from Chicago to Los Angeles and stay
with him and Ray at the house. People have been very generous and one
has had a lot of luck. The visit was amazing. Charles used to work in the
film industry, and they were friends with Billy Wilder, who was directing
the Marilyn Monroe film, *Some Like it Hot*. We went on the set. It's a
fantastic film, and funnier every year, because you suddenly understand
the jokes! Disneyland was new—that is, the little, original Disneyland.

Our relationship continued until Ray died. I went to visit him for the last
time [in 1979] the year after Charles died. But he lives on! The black
book is part of putting all their life's work in order. It's also interesting
that only one project that they had going before he died was continued—
everything else was stopped.

22 Peter Carter was a very faithful assistant to
Mies van der Rohe. He worked, I believe, inter alia
on the buildings in Toronto.

Did Alison leave anything for you to finish?

Yes. That is, she established the language for the German work—the Tecta Factory and the Axel Bruchhäuser house. It is a whole new mode—I know that puts it crudely. I've simply continued that. After fifteen years or so of continuing, I still have not exhausted that which Alison started. Your life works out like that: you find a theme that you think you can work with, and gradually you use it up. But Alison's theme is still becoming more complex.

I've just come back from Paris, where I saw the exhibition of [Jean] Dubuffet at the Centre Pompidou. In Paris someone asked me if I knew about this artist in the 1940s and if he had an influence on our work. Well, you never know; you never know the absolute origin of an idea.

The difficult thing is explaining the reciprocal nature of Alison's and my talents. We were totally different, professionally. That's fairly normal in a partnership. In an English public school, the school has the children throughout the day and is imprinting them with things beyond the home. It is the same when you live and work with somebody, you are with them twenty-four hours a day. It becomes a question of looking and reflecting on the notions of the other. You have time for it. With all the social things, like being prepared to do without money and having the children in ordinary schools, we were similar. We did not want to have to do something just to earn money to keep going.

I wonder how Paul Rudolph [23] felt about that. I always felt that until he was forty-five, he didn't ever do what he didn't want to do.

23 Paul Rudolph (1918–1997) was regarded by
Alison and Peter as the most promising American
architect in the period after World War II.

Alison and Peter
Smithson,
Hexenhaus
extensions
(1986–2001), Bad
Karlshaten, Germany.
Upper-floor plan,
Rosa Jackson, Peter
Smithson, and
Lorenzo Wong, 2001

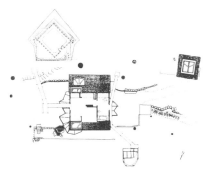

Alison had an arrangement to go to Florida to give a lecture in
November 1993, but it was obvious by springtime that she was going
to die. So I wrote and asked if I should come and substitute for her. I
went and I did what she had on her checklist, which included looking
at his early buildings. On my way back, I went to New York to see Paul
and show him my photographs of his projects. I said, "Look, Paul, this is
not so bad. Once you get to seventy-five, then things start to be really
rather rough." Then he said, "Do you know how old I am? Seventy-five."
It was a very nice visit. I don't think he had been back to look at his
early work, and it still looked good. One house had been restored, and
it was immaculate. The high school was also really rather good.[24]

The question we haven't answered is the business of why there's such
a rich relationship between the architects of my generation and those in
the United States: it is because of the scholarship business. The new
generation of American architects were all in Europe with scholarships,
and therefore they met the people of their own generation. It was very
bonding, because in your twenties you're at the stage that friendship
continues throughout your life.

24 Paul Rudolph, The Healy Cottage, Sarasota,
Florida (1948–50), and Sarasota High School
(1958–60).

Could you explain the ideas behind the conglomerate order? [25]

Yes I can, but it's long. At its simplest, it can be explained through a farm. On a farm, a stone wall between fields pens in but also shelters the sheep in the snow time. Each part of a structure needs to perform and encompass many tasks. [26] In our time, we thought this way of building should be developed. It is nonformal and does not use classical geometry. If you look out of the window, you can see a certain something that allows you to locate yourself, to look this way and that way. We have only done one substantial building that follows these ideas fully, and only one person in twenty-five million likes it! [27]

(Incidentally, I recently went to the AA to see this exhibition called *As Found*, [28] and as I was coming out, a Chinese girl said to me, "We're going next week to do a measured drawing of your building in Bath." Oh, that's fantastic.)

That's what conglomerate ordering is: to build it like a farmer when he's making a decision—"Well, if I have to do all that work, I also want it to do that and that and that." Everything should have multiple uses.

25 "For the feeling we experience of a fabric being 'ordered,' when we do not understand the place at a glance or do not know the building, we are using the words 'conglomerate ordering.'" Alison and Peter Smithson, "Conglomerate Ordering," in *Italian Thoughts*, 60.
26 "Such scrutiny is no more than was normal when making a farm, or a fortress, or a bridge, in the past; then, because of the effort, the hard work needed to make it, each part needed to perform and encompass many tasks; there had to be an interlock of actions, including the process of erection, even subsequent alteration. But to think like this now demands a conscious set of mind, for it is no longer normal; to think this can overturn our accepted notions of the arrangement of spaces and of the elements of supporting and servicing. Alison and Peter Smithson, "Think of it as a Farm," *Italian Thoughts*, 80.
27 Alison and Peter Smithson, Building 6 East, Architecture and Engineering Building, University of Bath, (1982–88).
28 *As Found* (Basel: Verlag Lars Müller, April, 2001).

When I was reading **Italian Thoughts,** *I was struck by a passage that says places draw us to them for reasons beyond the five senses.*[29] **What is the role of place in your design?**

That really is part of the conglomerate ordering business—not only the visual, but what a place smells like, how the wind hits it, and all that. The secondary aspect of conglomerate ordering is that if a thing is well-achieved but its use dies, its quality brings other things to it for which it is suitable.

An example I use is a Cambridge Courtyard, built in the Middle Ages for residential use. Because it was based on a monastery, it has certain qualities as a result. At the end of the academic year, the students put on performances and find a corner within the courtyard that has the right qualities for the play that they are performing—they are using its qualities. If a place serves a function well and appropriately, then it has a long life—other uses come to it.

29 "Places draw us to them for reasons beyond the feelings derived from the five senses... some deeper recognition is at work, felt through an unextinguishable animal sensibility." Alison and Peter Smithson, "Territory," in *Italian Thoughts*, 32.

Do you think that cities such as Phoenix can ever recover
from the extreme urban sprawl that has taken away its social
and emotional core, and what advice would you have for a city
such as this one?

You begin to think it is already developing in some way. In Phoenix you
have the "walling in"—the wall between the road and the communities.
It is rebuilding itself in some way, but it will never be a traditional city.
The traditional city is about hundreds of building and housing types
because there are many generations of buildings.

Phoenix only started out in the 1950s. That is just two generations ago,
and the quality of the construction is so low that the buildings won't
survive. This is not a result of things being built speculatively. Since the
1700s in Europe, buildings have been built speculatively. In Phoenix, this
is something else. We actually don't know anything about the people
who live in these houses here. What is their essential identity, and
where is it derived from? It might be that they've seen an advertisement
for a beautiful stainless-steel pot. That might be enough. It's where your
pleasures lie, isn't it?

For example, one of my children is now living in a town named Stamford.
It was very rich in the Middle Ages and there's a house called Burleigh
House—an Elizabethan house. It is like a palace. I suspect that is why
there are five very well-built churches in their town. The area was very

productive; Stamford cloth was well known in Venice in Henry III's reign [1216–1272]. What is so marvelous is that my child lives in a thing called Tower House, which is a Gothic Revival addition built onto a genuine Gothic underneath-part. In this town you can walk to everything within 200 meters—the grass-cutter repair, two butchers, and a vegetable market, all within five minutes. So everything is done on foot. Around this town, now, have sprung the usual suburbs, with supermarkets and so forth. I cannot imagine this type of city happening here; nothing will last long enough.

The Response to The Glut

Lecture by Peter Smithson

The following transcription is from Peter Smithson's lecture at ASU on 16 November 2001, and was assembled with his assistance prior to his death in 2003. The text printed in blue type was taken directly from Peter's lecture notes; the text in brown type is a transcription of Peter's conversation with the audience.

Peter Smithson, Put-
away Villa (1994–2000).
Drawing, collage, Ana
Iglesias González, and
Peter Smithson

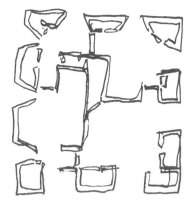

Alison and Peter
Smithson,
Cubical House
(1956–57). Plan,
Alison Smithson

For people with jobs, acquisition has increased by nearly ten times in the last twenty years; the living space available in the dwelling has been overwhelmed by not-at-present-in-use-maybe-never-again objects: baby stuff, cots, baby carriers, baby car-seats, prams, high-chairs, pampers by the pack, skate boards, roller skates, mountain bicycles, canoes.

These not-at-present-in-use-maybe-never-again objects are more or less dead storage, but there is also the live storage of clothing and accessories in daily use, and a third category, the storage of tools and equipment for the maintenance of the dwelling itself and for its objects.

For all of this, maybe 30 percent of a dwelling's volume is needed. Thus formative now to the idea of dwelling is the established need for storage. Formative also to the dwelling and the dwelling group is the established use of the motor-car to transport the objects stored, for the same thrust of industrialization has put the individual motor-car into every life and every landscape, just as it has put all those objects into the dwelling.

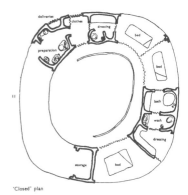

Alison and Peter Smithson, Appliance House (1957–58). Entrance elevation, "closed" plan, Alison Smithson

Entrance elevation

'Closed' plan

The intention of the Appliance House projects we made in the 1950s was to regain as much as possible of the house as usable space. In that period of just-ending scarcity of material goods, to get rid of the spatially intrusive welter of the then-noisy domestic machines into "Appliance Cubicles" could, it was thought, achieve this.

Not so now.

So the Appliance House was to contain the noisy appliances within containers, freeing the living space from the throbbing of the appliances.

You won't see much difference between what I am trying to say and what J. B. Jackson said.[1] That is, he noted the change in the domestic garage from chronicled observation. What I am trying for is an appropriate change, an organic change, in the plan of the house itself.

1 J. B. Jackson, "The Domestication of the American Garage," in *The Necessity for Ruins* (Amherst: The University of Massachusetts Press, 1980), 103.

Put-away Villa.
Plans, Lorenzo
Wong, 1994

GROUND FLOOR PLAN

We made a new study in late 1993–early 1994, which was worked on again in 2000, for a villa where storage generated the plan.

This Put-away Villa sets out the shape of the new need in the same way that Le Corbusier's villas set out his view of the new need at the end of the 1920s.

Le Corbusier's five points, with which I'm sure you are all familiar, contrasted the traditional house with his proposal. For me it is unbelievable that there was more tuberculosis in Stockholm before the First World War than anywhere else in Europe. It probably happened because of the density and the poor housing. The generation of Le Corbusier thought that architecture could be a tool for making a change.

It was Le Corbusier's Villa Garches (1927) which established the shape of the new need in the heroic period. Le Corbusier's five points of the new architecture—the pilotis, the roof garden, the free plan, the horizontal window, and the free facade—presented a shape for more fresh air and more exercise, a house arrangement to suit changing social habits.

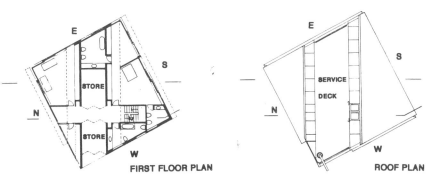

FIRST FLOOR PLAN

ROOF PLAN

So, with the Put-away Villa, we designed another kind of housing type that set out the need for our time in the same way Le Corbusier's villas set out his views of the needs of the 1920s.

At the heart of the plan at each level of the Put-away Villa is the large-item storage, available to every room without passing from another room. The core of the plan is storage, leaving the living rooms free. In addition, all rooms have cupboards for their specific day-to-day needs.

A service deck at roof-level is available both as a sundeck, sheltered by the sloping side-roofs so as to be out of sight from the ground, and as a work area for the maintenance of things in use and things stored. It serves as a secluded roof space, like a back yard.

Put-away Villa. Axiometric, Lorenzo Wong and Peter Smithson, 1994–2000

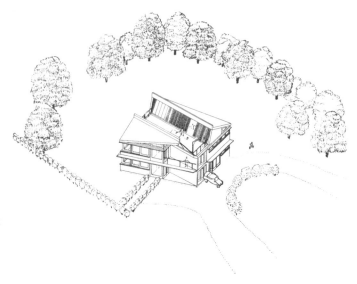

Put-away Villa. Aerial view, Lorenzo Wong and Peter Smithson, 1994–2000

Materials enter the house and can be distributed without disturbing the rooms. It is like a loading dock in a warehouse. The villa is designed for a supposed European client.

At the sides of the service deck, the rooms facing north have a south-facing roof light and the rooms facing south have a north-facing roof light. This service deck is used for household tasks: repairs to furniture, washing of carpets and hangings, bicycle cleaning and repairs, and so on. The faces of the roof lights are secured by lattice-screens, both against damage and against too easy observation of the activities in the rooms below. These lattice-screens are controlled with key access from above or adjusted by the occupants from the rooms below in order to see the stars or change light qualities in the room.

What is difficult to realize in Phoenix is that we are handling the sun in reverse. We're trying to get the warmth into the house rather than push it out. Any control system is to be able to look out to the sky.

As the floor levels of the axonometric drawings are filled with the things stored, one becomes aware of having re-invented the Edwardian (Wilhelmine) period middle-class house, with its flower arranging room, cutlery cleaning pantry, the servant rooms of the living rooms, and so on.

The difference, one supposes, being of intention.

In the Put-away Villa, as shown in the drawings, the living space is clear. The pieces of furniture remain themselves. Thus the maximum of space is available for the human drama: there is a sense of being protected in order to act.

You are all familiar with the interiors before the First World War, where everything was not itself, but was a support for something else.

Virginia Woolf wrote a biography of Elizabeth Barrett Browning's dog. Browning moved from a house in Bloomsbury to a house in Florence. The description that follows is of the dog's experience of the house in Florence:

"It was bare. All those draped objects of his cloistered and secluded days had vanished. The bed was a bed. The wash stand was a wash stand. Everything was itself, not another thing."[2]

What dominates the eye in these axonometrics are the storerooms, not the living rooms. You see, it's marvelous, because the things stored are multiple and familiar. The eye reads them more strongly than the empty rooms.

Put-away Villa.
Drawing, collage,
Ana Iglesias
González and Peter
Smithson,
1994–2000

2 Virginia Woolf, *Flush* (New York: Harcourt, Brace, 1933), 128.

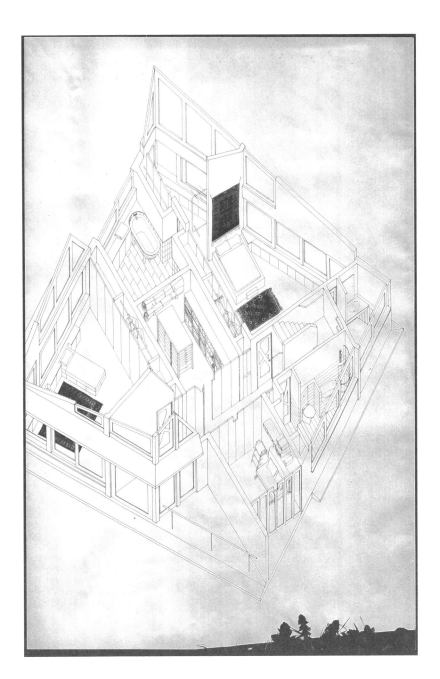

Now in Elizabethan times in England (the 1500s), the grand houses of the newly hyper-rich had a long gallery for walking and talking when the weather was bad, as well as for the display of paintings.

In Hardwick New Hall there is a gallery which runs along the whole extent of the house. What's nice about this drawing is that it indicates the thick spine wall, where the fireplaces are, as well as the heating apparatus and the perimeter bay windows that let in the light. In the wintertime the family would pull back to the fireplaces. The organization of the house was based on the available coal. In this part of England coal was produced at the time. Fuel found formal expression in the organization of houses, so that in the winter you have screens around the gallery against the fireplaces, and in the summer you moved into the bay windows. The organization of the plan was a consequence of thinking about the way that it could be used—that is, the pleasures of winter and summer. You see, the long gallery is at the top of the house.

These were fantastically rich people. The new middle class. Hardwick's owner was Elizabeth Shrewsbury. She was rather like Elizabeth Taylor. She had four husbands, all of whom died.

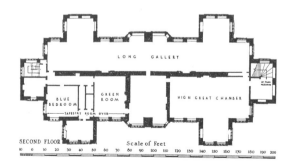

Robert Smythson,
Hardwick Hall (1590).
Second floor plan

Peter Smithson,
rridor (1998–99),
ecta, Lauenförde.
Photograph, Peter
Smithson, 2000

In Elizabethan times paintings were rarities. They were very few.
Today there is a glut. Many.

In the vast new halls of art galleries full of new paintings and art
manifestations, people walk, talking little, paying only fragmentary
attention to all they are passing. Just as tourists now pass the shrines
of Saints and churches, they pass in the same way before the objects
in art galleries.

In the Put-away Villa there is the opportunity for bareness itself to be
a quality to be sustained or revived by the process of putting away.

Loggia at the
Casa de Pilatos,
Seville, Spain.
Photograph,
Peter Smithson,
1997

In a house in Seville, Spain—the Casa de Pilatos—there is an empty
room and an empty loggia, which somehow has the quality of emptiness
that I am trying to define. I was overwhelmed. This is the quality that
emptiness can bring. In its way it was fulfillment—which is a ridiculous
word to use—the fulfillment of the emptiness.

Bringing out for the seasons—much in winter, little in summer.

Bringing out for festivals—of the church, or of the family.

Putting away for renewals, putting away for sadness.

Thinking about it now, the empty room is the same as the empty stage.
You furnish it with those things necessary.

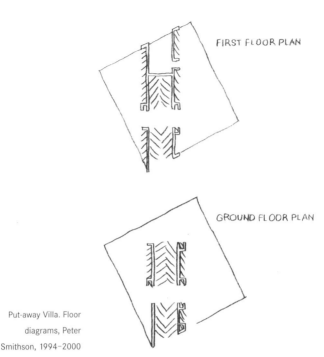

FIRST FLOOR PLAN

GROUND FLOOR PLAN

Put-away Villa. Floor
diagrams, Peter
Smithson, 1994–2000

*You might ask, "why is he worrying about children's parties or an aunt
dying and what you do for them?" Because that's what the house is for.
That's it. And the emptiness is achievable by a way of storing the objects.
In the Two Gantries House, that is in essence what is happening.*

Peter Smithson,
House with Two
Gantries (1977).
Photomontage, Peter
Smithson and Lorenzo
Wong, 1977

The House with Two Gantries was intended for a man like me, who sometimes wishes he could put things away easily that he is not at the moment using, a man in a family who gets things out for festivals and homecomings and wants to put them away afterward. For a family who likes to decorate their house, this house allows them to do just that. They can move things easily from room to room or put them away.

Should there perhaps be art galleries like this?

The storage area of the art gallery could have even more volume than the display galleries, with access to archive material made easier than is usual in art galleries. (Not to be too casual about the difficulties with rare paintings).

So the program for the Put-away Art Galleries is similar to the Put-away Villa. In the time of glut it would be wonderful for the gallery rooms to be, for reason, empty. The galleries empty.

I once wanted to find a picture by Francesco di Giorgio Martini that I knew was in a gallery in Florence, and I asked them if I could go into the archives to find it. They sent a person with me and we took it to the window—you're not allowed to put light on pictures. I had fifteen minutes, absorbing the picture in a completely different way, alone. A Put-away Art Gallery would be completely different.

Within the dwelling zone, the only one which I had seen that had the qualities I was looking for was within a courtyard with an open space in the middle with children, and you could say that was because the culture of this open space was a different culture than that of the glut culture.

The efficiency of the production of the United States makes the notion of the empty room an enemy of the economy—things have to be born to keep the machine running. You can do something about the restoration of quality to space and to things in your own circumstances. You can ask "is it possible to do it professionally, to get this quality so that other people can observe it?" and maybe these people will be in some part of your culture which prefers being like Elizabeth Barrett Browning's dog, who clearly enjoyed an empty room—people removed from the glut culture into another culture and finding it enjoyable. So maybe you have to culture your path and set yourself to recover space and the notion of emptiness.

The qualities I found in that loggia might be something within that.

Put-away Addendum.

To put-away is of course an instinct in oneself. For me, to be able to see one thing at a time, the territory has to be clear.

It has been wrong to separate pictures and artifacts from their owners and their places—in churches, in houses—to preserve their singleness and their rarity.

One is oneself guilty. So much better to take in, instead of looking whilst talking of something else—to ask if one may come back later, just to look again in private.

Conversation 3

Footnotes by Peter Smithson unless otherwise noted. —*Eds*.

Peter Smithson, Front
Door Porch (1998),
Hexenhaus, Bad
Karlshafen, Germany.
Photograph, Peter
Smithson, 1999

Chisenhale Road.
Photograph, Nigel
Henderson, 1951

I was thinking about your lecture when you described us as the generation of the "too much."[1] You said that the galleries should be empty, and I found this idea to be fantastic. Could you say more about this?

It is an incredible idea, isn't it? In the 1940s and 1950s in Europe, there was little to buy, whereas today it is the opposite. Then, there were very few artifacts, and now there are too many. Therefore, what is the job of the architect to respond to the "too much"? But that question in itself is a Puritan way of looking at it. Is it right to have so much? Can we get the quality out of almost nothing? The quality of emptiness?

They can achieve that on the stage, can't they? Somehow, they can have a production in which the emptiness of the stage is the quality of it.

1 See lecture "Response to the Glut" in this
book, 52. —*Eds.*

Could you suggest how we are to obtain the "fulfillment of emptiness"?

Certainly. You could continue the conversation we had in the street about making a network.[2] Imagine a walkway six meters across; then you come to a place that is four meters across; then you suddenly come to a piece that is eight or nine meters across, containing nothing. Before you move on to the next section, you are suddenly brought up, not with a shock of something exciting, but with a shock of nothing. It is a very professional way of looking at space. The developer is not going to be very fond of that, is he?

The analogy that was being drawn in the lecture was the way in which Quaker meetings[3] invest the space between the sitting people. That empty space becomes the church. That creates a format—a ritual, I suppose you could call it—which sanctifies emptiness. You have to go to a Quaker meeting to experience it. We now have very few; I was astonished to read that there are only 55,000 Quakers in England. When the movement was at its peak, there were hundreds of thousands.

2 See page 34 in this book. *—Eds.*
3 "At the base was the local meeting with its worshipping congregation. The popular picture of a plain-garbed group sitting silently in an unornamented room is correct. Such mundane affairs as seeing that the meeting house was cleaned, firewood provided, and broken glass replaced were entrusted to preparative meetings. Most large local meetings were preceded by preparatory meetings, which could settle minor offenses and appoint overseers to report any violations of the discipline to the monthly meeting." Hubert Lidbetter, *The Friends Meeting House* (York: William Sessions Limited, 1979), 15. *—Eds.*

What do you think of the minimalist art movement relative to the idea of emptiness?

I really have very little experience of it. There are some shops in Knightsbridge, near Harrods; they are the smart, expensive shops that have been done by young architects. They are very nice, actually, and appear to be made out of almost nothing. I would say that this type of architecture is a bit cult-like— that is to say you need a specialized audience. The emptiness I'm talking about should not need a specialized audience. Think of the ordinary person walking through one of these spaces with a small child: would she have any experience of this sort of space? Probably not.

Thinking back to the lecture, who were the people in the 1920s that built the Villas Garches and Savoy? They were rich people, the Jewish intellectuals of Gertrude Stein's social class. These houses were probably not received at all by ordinary people. What would ordinary people have to say about these villas now? It is the same: they would not be understood. It is the same situation with our client Axel Bruchhäuser. He is an extraordinary man, not an ordinary man. Axel is a client who knows as much as you do about history, but he doesn't know the secrets of the discipline, and that's why he comes to you.

You could ask what does one do with this lecture about emptiness, and the answer is that you have to go out and try not to make it. You could say there's no point in a lecture or a discourse unless it is an offering.

Maybe I can take up this question—this challenge—to locate this place of emptiness. In this country it seems that nature, broadly put, performs that function of emptiness. There's a tradition, a postwar tradition, when everybody had cars and took the family out to nature, out to the national parks. That was an experience that every family would enjoy together. It would be an experience that young children would remember and it would have a tremendous impact on them. It was not an experience that one would find within the city, but rather one that you left the city for.

There is enough territory in the U.S. for that, to go out and acquire emptiness. I once had the experience myself here in America, after school holidays. The camping sites were empty, so you would go to a national or regional park and be there alone with the Grand Tetons and all that. Well, that sensibility, of course, was inventive, romantic—Ruskin[4] and all that lot.

The discourse with nature that takes place then began to replace religion. Nature became the godhead. Maybe this idea of emptiness is as I've made the analogy with the Quaker's space. It is a religious form in a way. Why did the Reformation happen? Because the reformers said that there was too much going on in the church and we needed to simplify.

4 John Ruskin (1819–1900), was an artist, scientist, poet, environmentalist, philosopher, and art critic. Ruskin's letter to *The Times* in 1851, supporting the much-derided Pre-Raphaelites for their naturalism and truth to nature, marked a turning point in their perception by the public. John Ruskin, *The Seven Lamps of Architecture* (New York: Farrar, Stratus and Giroux, 1988). —*Eds.*

Minimalism began in America in the mid-1960s and 1970s. One of its strong motifs is that it brings nature into the gallery or, vice versa, to bring the gallery sensibility out to nature. There was a lot of back and forth in that regard—for example, Michael Heizer[5] filled a gallery full of dirt. Emptying out the gallery of any use other than simply contemplating the dirt was a way of creating, in Manhattan, a space of emptiness and contemplation. That seems to have evolved or transformed itself into a minimalists chic, which has become a style. The question in my mind is how that tradition, which indeed begins with Ruskin, transforms itself. When it becomes a question of merchandising, it is no longer attached to spiritual dimensions. I don't know how or exactly where it is supposed to get reinvigorated.

Minamilism is undoubtedly now marketed as a style.

What about your house in the country that we know from your book The Upper Lawn.[6] *The book explains the life of the house over a long period of time and constant change. Would you say that the progress of the house comes out of these qualities of emptiness you are speaking of?*

5 Michael Heizer (1944–), born to a family of geologists, encouraged his fascination with mysterious sites marked by evidence of ancient technology, such as the shifting of huge stones. See Germano Celant, *Michael Heizer* (Milan: Fondazione Prada, 1997). *—Eds.*
6 Alison and Peter Smithson, *The Upper Lawn Solar Pavilion Folly* (Barcelona: UPC Editions, 1983). *—Eds.*

Alison and Peter Smithson,
Upper Lawn (1959–1982),
Fonthill, England. Garden
front section with well, Peter
Smithson, 1975.

I've been thinking about that house recently because a Swiss man has done a new book about it.[7] Undoubtedly it's a work of another nature. But still, it is a true Brutalist work. That is, the old walls, the wood, the stainless steel, the aluminum skin, the teak—all the materials— are used so that you feel their quality. But again, you're working for yourself. For example, in the bathroom there were the stone walls of the old house. At first we ran the pipework on the surface of the masonry. Later, we buried it, because when you got to use it you found the expo- sure of the pipe-work quite an irritation because of the condensation— something you do not have in Phoenix. So it is the second process in which you take out conflicting elements. This sort of process is very much like stage design: once you start to run rehearsals and things don't work, you pull them out or change the lighting.

7 Bruno Krucker, *Complex Ordinariness* (Zürich:
gta, 2002). –*Eds*.

I like the way you put the idea of emptiness in a hypothesis, because in a way it opens space for our generation to explore these ideas. I've been thinking that it is more than emptiness that we need to consider, and about what Heidegger says about the essence of the space.[8] *Do you think that is the way our architecture is going? We know how to make buildings, but do we know how to make them in a way in which that emptiness is filled and uses the material or an element of construction?*

At a joke level, you could say that you don't get paid for the little bit that is empty. But there's a whole other level to consider: back to the Quakers' meeting space, there is all this empty space and just a row of chairs—virtually a row of rectangular chairs that you get from the Salvation Army. There is no formal content at all. It is only when people sit in the chairs that there is content.

The big churches of Palladio in Venice[9] are made of masonry—at least where it is "important"; the steps are made of six-meter single pieces of stone. That is an enormous dimension. The church was prepared to invest in quality, and the emptiness engages with this quality. The emptiness implies an architecture of the poor, as when architecture doesn't cost the person anything. This brings the role of the architect much closer to being that of an evangelical priest—that is, he's not working for money. This issue of money came up in one of the previous questions.[10] What is the relationship between your work and family? Does your family have to be prepared to make sacrifices? Well, I don't think they did.

8 Martin Heidegger (1889–1976) developed the idea of *Gelassenheit*, which he meant as a state of mind of letting things be. To acheive this state, one needed to be in a place where "the play between thing and nothing could be sensed." See Martin Heidegger, *Being and Time* (San Francisco: Harper, 1962), 14. *—Eds.*
9 The Church of San Giorgio Maggiore (1560–80) and Church of Il Redentore (1576–91).
10 See page 30 in this book. *—Eds.*

The other thing about being poor is that you could say you are sacrificing for the rest of the community. In our culture, where many things are provided by the state, if you don't have an income and are not paying any income tax, it is like you are living off of everybody else. The children's school fee, the fire department, the Town Hall that sanctifies marriage—they are all public services paid for out of taxation. If you are not paying any taxes, you are freeloading. Everything is much more complicated. But this route we are going along now is too difficult to think about. You work by making a simple decision. You tend not to think it through.

I am talking about doing what seems necessary. What seems necessary may not give any money.

What do you think our culture can learn from cultures that are relatively in tact and hold emptiness at the core of their belief system? Certain Asian cultures have the idea of emptiness within everything—daily life, ritual, building, architecture. How can we use their idea of emptiness without superficially copying it?

Well, if you take from those cultures, it is yet another form of eclecticism, isn't it? It has to come from you, somehow. You could say almost the opposite: if you go to a place where it moves you deeply, you should almost take a vow not to copy it.

A fantastic example is when Christianity was moved to make a cathedral as the biggest gift to God that they could think of, and then they would fill it with people. It is such a fantastic idea. But when one makes a little one out of cardboard, maybe it is still a gift.

My experience in South America was in Brazil. There the churches are indebted to European architecture. But they are not like European architecture; they are evolved from it. Maybe that was part of the Iberian gift. Their priesthood did not impose themselves on native culture. They did it cleverly, melding together the native sensibilities with what they were trying to introduce.

In regard to method, do you respond more to the positive or negative aspects of the given situation?

The only thing I can think of to reply to that is that there is a conscious attempt to build an alternative architecture—not that what the alternative architecture offers is always useful. For example, there is a school of architecture in Chile that builds things on the beach.[11] These things are perfectly useless day-to-day. They represent a counter-form. That doesn't seem to me to be terribly useful. I think at worst the space of the building, of the room, has to be useable, particularly if you take the position that the space you make has to offer itself for the inventions of those who occupy it. In a way, what I am explaining is like a children's party. The mother organizes certain possibilities for play, but whether the party goes well or not depends on the invention of the children. The mother is designing a framework.

It might be in your nature to think you've got to destroy in order to build. Most revolutions have an aspect of destruction. An interesting thought is whether the United States in the twenty-first century is moving toward a revolution when the political movement of the right will tend to be entirely disruptive like Spain in 1936–38.[12]

11 Escuela de Arquitectura y Diseno, Universidad Catolica de Valparaiso, Chile. *—Eds.*
12 The Spanish Civil War was the culmination of a series of uneven struggles between the forces of reform and reaction which dominated Spain since 1908. See Paul Preston, *The Spanish Civil War* (London: Fontana Press, 1996), 10. *—Eds.*

How do you as an architect know when you have captured the idea of a project in the design? I remember a basic drawing exercise that required you to draw until you passed the best moment of the work. How do you recognize that moment in your work?

It is such a relief once you have found the line that holds the project. Usually you can work for days and days and days and get nowhere. Then you suddenly strike it. I think that often it happens accidentally. If you continue drawing, suddenly two lines come together and remind you of something. It is by chance. You can see it in almost everyone's work. If you look at the work of Louis Kahn, for example, he goes from fantastic drawings to terrible drawings, not getting anything. And then it is there.

It happens through the element of ordinary work. A person working with a type of circuitry suddenly realizes that this piece connected with that piece does that. There is always an element of chance.

But I hate it when you are completely stuck, day after day and you can't find anything. That is usually the point in which eclecticism begins. You say, "I will take this from somebody else's work." Maybe it is a conventional thing. Nobody actually becomes themselves until the beginning of their forties, even great architects. Take Mies's Berlin houses for example.[13] He was born in 1886. It fits more or less—he was fortyish.

---

13 Brick Country House (1923) and Wolf House (1926). *–Eds.*

Alison and Peter Smithson,
The Economist Building
(1959–64), London.
Axonometric, Christopher
Woodward

*So you are learning from other people, and then what happens
when you get to be forty?*

Suddenly you discover what you want to do.

There is now a completely different set of circumstances, insofar as
machine drawing is the norm in ordinary offices: you are losing the contact between the pen and product. That is not necessarily bad, but
it has to be shown to be something good, which brings us back to the
question about models.[14]

I said that Mies made one-to-one models because with the one-to-one
model you can feel the physical quality, what it is going to be. But of
course it changes when it is the real material. If it is a rolled steel mem-
ber, it has a rather different quality than the wooden model. When they
had the Sir John Soane exhibition,[15] they reproduced the soft vaults that
Soane used. Of course, they were built originally in a kind of Roman
manner with pots—hollow ceramic pots in the depth of the vault. The
acoustic quality that resulted from these domes was utterly different
from the acoustic quality of those just made of plaster on metal lathing.

14 See page 40 in this book. *–Eds*.
15 John Soane, Architect: Master of Space and
Light, Royal Acadamy, London, September
11–December 3, 1999. Sir John Soane
(1753–1837) is the forgetter of the sacredness of
classical grammar.

Is the idea of emptiness related to the idea of an architecture without rhetoric?[16]

I am usually talking about things I am trying to do. Our assistant, Lorenzo Wong, made the statement that in a Japanese house there is no space left except inside the refrigerator. Going back to the lecture, there is a primative thought encompassed in Lorenzo's famous one-liner: the ordinary person's house is completely full of junk. Then you say, well that's stupid, we should find a way of controlling the junk, as they do in an office.

In Le Corbusier's time, he thought there were defects in the city that he wanted to correct,[17] and he thought about how to reformulate it. Well, the problem of the ordinary house is a similar thing. You must have a place to get rid of certain equipment of the house in order to do this or that, so that there is enough space that you can move a table about. This goes back to the simple things, like having empty space for children's parties so they don't break anything.

Another example is containing the cooking so that it doesn't smell and destroy the space. In an ordinary kitchen without an exhaust system, cooking destroys the space because the smell lingers. You think, "why don't I try to figure out a way of controlling that?" You give the space back. None of this is aimed at an exclusive client; neither was Le Corbusier aiming at a high level of design for rich people only. But it always turns out that only the rich people can afford this type of work.

16 See Alison and Peter Smithson, *Without Rhetoric. —Eds.*
17 See Le Corbusier, *The Radiant City* (New York: Orion Press, 1967).

Peter Smithson, Tea-
House (1998),
Hexenhaus, Bad
Karlshafen.
Photograph, Axel
Bruchhäuser, 1998

Our work in Germany[18] is exactly like this: the client said, "I'm lying in bed on the floor between six and seven o'clock in the morning, and the sun is coming in a certain direction; should I remodel the house so that I can enjoy the moment the sun is coming through?" Only a rich person can do this. When they say make this tiny change, four, five, six men come in, and as they touch the old house it fills with a cloud of dust. You have to have somebody clean up. An ordinary person will not do something like that. It's such a big upset in one's life.

Like in Catherine's little house,[19] she says to me, "if we had such and such, and the dog could run from there to there, that would be marvelous." But you don't do it because you don't have the money, the time, or the clean-up capacity. So in the end it all sounds very pessimistic. You often end up actually carrying out operations for really rich people. Not necessarily really rich people because that is another thing, but people like the Gertrude Stein family. The Garches, for example, were people of a certain social class; they were not really that rich. They were the children of a hardware storeowner. In European terms, not at all interesting, but moneyed. Even Frank Lloyd Wright, though he made designs for small houses—such as in the 1930s where there are four houses linked together with a cross wall—that could have been for lower-middle class, but most of his buildings were for rich people.

18 The extentions and buildings for Tecta and
Axel Bruchhäuser. *—Eds.*
19 House of Catherine Spellman. *—Eds.*

When you spoke about making a drawing and leaving space for the element of chance and accidental relationships, I wonder if surrealism ever influenced your work.[20]

If we continue the business of the house for the ordinary family, usually there is hardly the money to build the volume you want without extra things. What I said about the domestication of the American garage is that you don't build more space, you just fill the garage.[21] You take the car out. That was the move to create something new. All those corny things like little workshops would be moved out of the house and into the garage. The garage could accept the dirtiness.

We have two projects currently under construction. One is a kind of pavilion for this famous Axel Bruchhäuser.[22] This pavilion really isn't for anything—just to celebrate a circumstance. It took its starting point from a common experience but in an uncommon place.

If you think about the Philip Johnson glass-wall house,[23] in the evening, the architecture's space is defined by the floodlighting on the trees, and this house of Axel's is completely covered by really old trees. They are huge. Therefore there is a possibility, as it were, of making a pavilion in which the inside light goes out of all the walls and the roof. The Johnson house is a type of sandwich. The Lantern Pavilion is a kind of basket out of which light comes. It serves no function. You can think of things to use it for, but its prime intention is formal; it is exploring a possibility of the trees to be the enclosure.

20 See page 82 in this book. *—Eds.*
21 See page 53 in this book. *—Eds.*
22 Lantern Pavilion (2000–2001). *—Eds.*
23 Philip Johnson, Glass House, New Canaan, Conn. (1949). *—Eds.*

Park in Winter.
Photograph, Andre
Kertész, 1954

One last question, what do you think should be done with the World Trade Center site?

It's interesting to think about. All that land lies empty for you. One of the most primitive ideas is that it should be a memorial park. Central Park, now, is really beautiful after 150 years of growth. There is this sense of emptiness there. You can walk alone there. You can think in Central Park. As soon as you get into the real downtown you are bombarded with noise. You never thought there would be space to be alone downtown. Whether the space of the World Trade Center is big enough, I don't know. Once you are in the middle of Central Park, the buildings around the edge are a kind of profile. That is marvelous.

10 Richter Scale

Essay by Catherine Spellman and Karl Unglaub

Peter had shown us an empty room with a loggia in Spain. He said "the fulfillment of the emptiness" was apparent in these spaces. You could see that these
spaces were old, used, and adaptable to many functions. The material quality was
rich with color and texture but not consuming or very memorable. The spaces
were empty but full of potential. This type of space is common in many of Peter
and Alison Smithson's works, where a change of season or routine of daily life
alters the quality of the space. It was their intention to make spaces that could
accept changing activity and time. "Life occurs in the emptiness," Peter told us—a
thought, an intuition, and the wisdom of objective experience. One can only
imagine that making emptiness is making room, both literally and figuratively, in
which to live and think.

When and where did the Smithsons begin to become conscious of the qualities
of emptiness? We can find it in their built work, but it is not explicitly talked
about in their writings, although they do hint at it over and again. In *Urban
Structuring*[1] we find an image from the 1950s of Jackson Pollock painting in
his studio on a big empty surface on the floor, waving his brush in the air. The
movement of paint over the floor carries his expression. The lines on the canvas
are layered into a net, a lattice of color. The space of the painting is formed
between the layers of the colors. It is the space that makes these swirls of pigment a painting. This space is made with material of very specific qualities that
change when they are laced together. The phenomena of emptiness that one
finds in Pollock's paintings is hard to describe but absolutely exists. If one looks
long enough and hard enough, the canvas and pigment become magical and
full of light, air, and silence.

At the same time in the 1950s, the Smithsons' collaborator, Eduardo Paolozzi,
walked through the streets of Bloomsberry collecting books and printing simple
patterns for his collages. Today in Edinburgh, his studio at the National Galleries

1 Alison and Peter Smithson, *Urban Structuring*
(New York: Reinhold Publishing Corporation,
1967), 34.

of Scotland is overcrowded with found objects and remnants of materials saved
to weave together in future works. The eye to discover these things is his most
vital tool in the making of his work. His movements that cut, tear, and glue
the fragments together are very small, controlled, and precise. His collages are
constructed with the shapes of these found and processed materials and with the
space left empty between these materials. It is this repetitive and carefully posi-
tioned space that enables the viewer to experience the depth and richness
of the collage. This approach toward the "space between" is not dissimilar to the
space within the mat-buildings that the Smithsons started to work with in the
Berlin Hauptstadt competition in 1957, the Economist Building in 1959–64, and
explored with great intensity in the Government Offices for Kuwait in 1970. In
these projects the Smithsons' intention was to "move away from the individually
designed block towards a fabric of controlled and subtle repetition, such as the
multitude of domes that cover the Aleppo Bazaar, or the intricate geometric pat-
terned tiles of Isfahan."[2]

Simultaneously, their friend Nigel Henderson photographed children playing,
people shopping, and other scenes of everyday life in the Bethnal Green
neighborhood of London. The photographs show people moving within the space
of the street—a space clearly defined and regulated but not restrictive. The
photographs show how the streets were able to adapt to the changing needs and
desires of urban life, accommodating spontaneous activities and providing space
for people to live. It was during this time that the Smithsons suggested a new
concept for the urban house—one that would start with a new conception of the
street. As well, they took on the as-found social and physical qualities of the
working-class street life as a reference point. In their view, architecture and
urbanism are united through human associations that occur in space. Given
this point of view, it is logical that they would look to street life to conceive of
the new housing solutions that are presented in the Golden Lane Housing

2 Alison and Peter Smithson, *Works and Projects*,
ed. Marco Vidotto (Barcelona: Gustavo Gili,
1997), 138.

competition in 1952, the House of the Future exhibition in 1955–56, and at Robin Hood Gardens in 1966–72.

It is hard to say how these influences affected the Smithsons' early work. Peter suggested that it was more unconscious than anything else. "Relationships to people and ideas are formed around common interests, attractions, and time," he said. "It all melds together when one begins to design."[3] Look at the Hunstanton Secondary School, the Smithsons' first large project, built in 1949–54. Many of the widely published construction photographs reveal their fascination with the type of layered space we see in their visual references. The steel structure is a lattice of material, brilliantly organized and detailed. Within this web of sinuous material is the space for the workings of the school. These photographs show the abstract quality of the project. Light, shadow, and reflection dematerialize the structure, leaving pure space. One could wonder what one would do in these spaces, and that seems to be the effect that the Smithsons were hoping for. They describe the project as having two lives: "an everyday life of teaching children, noise, furniture, and chalk dust.... And a secret life of pure space, the permanent built form which will persist when school has given way to museum or warehouse."[4]

Additionally, it is important to remember the Smithson's relationship to the Team 10 group, which inherited the ideals of modernism and urbanism that were established by Le Corbusier and CIAM. Team 10 sought to resolve the problem of relating architecture to the city and the city to human life. With the Hunstanton School in their pocket and Team 10 conversations in the air, the Smithsons designed their first evocative urban project for Berlin in 1957. The Hauptstadt was a network of connections in both plan and section that offered a new way to move through the city. Spaces in which to gather and socialize were left between the walkways and connectors. Here again the abstract qualities of a spatial lattice are present, only this time at a much larger scale. These spaces differ greatly

3 Peter Smithson, conversation with authors, November, 2001.
4 Peter and Alison Smithson, *The Charged Void: Architecture* (New York: Monacelli Press, 2001), 42.

from space in urban situations reserved for parks or playing fields. These spaces are instead free for the chosen activities of their users. Their identities change with the type of activity, time, season, and even emotion. When these spaces fill they become "charged"—to use Peter's word—with the values and complexity of the group.

The Smithsons' thoughts about urban space, first sketched in the Hauptstadt project, are refined in Robin Hood Gardens and the Economist Building. In both of these projects, the spaces between the built structures have received much attention. These spaces are consciously left empty with the idea that they would be filled with constantly changing human activity. In the most positive way, these spaces deal with what is often considered an urban problem: emptiness. In the modern city, undesignated space has often been labeled with negative terms such as vacant, marginal, or abandoned. Yet the Smithsons have recognized that these spaces in fact provide something essential—flexibility and room to accommodate the differing natures of society.

Architectural space is difficult to describe, record, or comprehend, and real insight about it is sometimes offered unconsciously. About the urban space left at the Economist Building, Peter has said it "makes a new sort of spatial quality . . . and although certain spatial qualities were consciously sought, what is there on the ground is more than that sought for."[5] Perhaps emptiness was not explicitly in mind in these early projects, but certainly what was built captures the ideas of empty space that Peter spoke about. The urban life of the Economist Building, for social rather than architectural reasons, has seen better use than that at Robin Hood Gardens. Nonetheless, both projects successfully integrate themselves into the existing fabric, make a clear statement about new ways of considering two established building types (office and housing), and make an intermediate empty space that enhances the patterns of movement in the city.

5 Peter and Alison Smithson, *The Charged Void: Architecture*, 278.

Several times Peter has referred to the Quakers to elaborate on his discussion of emptiness. The Quakers are also known as "seekers" and "friends," which are terms that are also applicable to Team 10 and the Independent Group, which the Smithsons were very involved with in the 1950s. Coming out of a long period of reformation in seventeenth-century Europe, the Quakers were questioning the standards and authority in society of religion, hoping to reestablish essential values and obtain a more direct contact with and experience of God by removing the excess or, in Peter's words, "the too much," that was going on in the church and everyday life. A close look at the rituals and ceremonies of the Quakers reveals an even more direct example of emptying. The maintenance of "quietness" in their religious and everyday life is an attempt to keep human intrusions from cluttering mental and physical space. Their architecture avoids symbolism, self-expression, and decoration. Instead, their buildings express utility and simplicity.

In Quaker literature one finds frequent use of the word "presence." At once both vague and suggestive, the word embraces the tension between two forms of work: product and process, noun and verb. Unconcerned with the distinction between the active (to present) and passive (being present) meanings of the word, the Quaker community is interested in the play and tension between something and nothing. Recall the common allegory of "the jug." When filling a jug, it is the emptiness that holds the fluid. Therefore, the utility that the potter makes is the nothing of the jug. The juxtaposition of opposites, dissolution of subject matter, general absence of individuality, making something from nothing— these are the characteristics of "presence" that are also found throughout the Smithsons' work. Reviewing their movement between emptiness and activity might be a key to understanding these qualities in their work—after all, this back-and-forth dynamic is central to their process.

Consider their early exhibition work, Patio and Pavilion (1956) and the House of the Future (1955–56).[6] Both projects use the idea of a courtyard to organize the space, however they do so in completely different ways. The Patio and Pavilion places the built elements in the center of the open space, making the material the subject of the exhibition piece, while the House of the Future builds around the open space, making the space the subject. One offers a new concept of modern urban dwelling by bringing the garden into the house, while the other reconsiders an ancient prototype, the primitive hut. One exploits the qualities of "ordinary" building materials, while the other explores what was at that time "high-tech."

Following this back-and-forth criteria, the Smithsons continued with a series of projects that measured the possibilities of fibers, lattice, and trees. In idea and form these projects are about wavelike layers of material and space that together create places for light, shadow, air, and inhabitation. The Wokingham Infant School of 1958, for example, starts like a cluster of twigs that have fallen in such a way as to form an enclosure. One piece touches the next, suggesting a continuous wave of movement that could reach into the adjoining neighborhood. In plan and in section one finds reference to the growth and structure of a tree. One could say that here children grow under the space of the tree. The Economist Buildings of 1959–64 invert the tree fabric of the school, sheltering the plaza space from the activity of the street while simultaneously making a passage through the block. Here, fiberlike voids between the built structure create a flowing screen, which appears to be more solid than void, defining the empty public space in between.

The British Embassy project for Brasilia in 1964–68 was designed to be a solid linear fiber between two sinuous stripes of landscapes. Here the building planes rise out of the ground plane, uniting the two in a type of braid. These layers

6 Patio and Pavilion appeared in This is
Tomorrow, White Chapel Art Gallery, London,
1956; House of the Future appeared in Ideal
Home, Olympia, London, 1955–56.

provide the inhabitant with shelter, privacy, and protection from the wind, light, and air. They have the effect of extending the project to the horizon, dissolving the visitor's ability to measure the limit or scale of the project. With the Garden Building for St. Hilda's College in Oxford (1967–70), the Smithsons vacillate back to building as an object placed carefully in a space—or so it would seem from the site plan. Again they consider the structure of a tree, which now takes the form of a layered facade screen that surrounds the solid volume. This has the effect of dissolving the objectness of the plan and allows the project to grow up from the ground in a way similar to the old tree that first occupied the site.

The ideas behind the mat-building have a presence in a variety of juxtaposed ways in many of the projects of the 1970s and early 1980s. The proposal for the Government Offices in Kuwait, for example, is a mat-building on a larger scale than the Economist Building. Here however, the weblike facade elements that provide sun protection are devices with more differentiated, functional, and spatial considerations than the earlier mat-building projects. The organization of the section is more diverse, and public space is entirely within the voids that are between, under, and within the building. Lucas Headquarters, built in 1973–74, is a type of lattice placed within trees. Again it is the facade that holds the space and prepares the place for the building. The recesses of the plan, which could be considered a mat-plan, push the building between the trees. The Pahlavi National Library for Tehran, built four years later, works with the voids of the light. The volumes of the building are more solid than the earlier projects, which allows them to catch and direct the light very precisely. Here the clear solid/void definition of a mat-building is less visible.

From 1978 to 1983, Alison and Peter Smithson worked at the University of Bath on five related projects. Here they developed the idea of mat-buildings into another direction with a wider perspective. Their projects interconnect the existing campus buildings by finding and following the natural pathways within the campus. Formed by gathering together a number of dissimilar materials, elements, and programs, these buildings represent the Smithsons' definition of conglomerate: "Conglomerate ordering harnesses all the senses. It can happily operate with a certain roughness; it can operate at night; it can offer, especially, pleasures beyond those of the eyes."[7] At the University of Bath, parts and pieces are organized within structural systems that carry the weight of the buildings and are detailed to operate as shading devices, water-shedding mechanisms, and circulation systems. In contrast to the tendency of the time, these buildings do not hide the complexity of the building. Rather, they celebrate and express that complexity with very controlled and precise placement of building elements and the open spaces between them. The fragile lattice layers of multiple meanings of the 1970s seem to have clashed together and become solid, or they disappeared and opened the space for inhabitation—the conglomerate.

This perspective allowed the Smithsons to design some even more radical projects over the next decade: Parc de la Villette, Paris, in 1982; Wilde Wege-Wild Ways, Berlin, in 1988; Bibliotheca Alexandria in 1989; and Acropolis Place, Athens, in 1990. Parc de la Villette is layered out of water zones, picnic greens, and exhibition gardens, latticed in between trees, grass, water, and the sky, and protected by a solid edge. Peter described it as a "growing tapestry of planting."[8] The plan resembles an oriental carpet with its melded figure and field pattern. Even more immaterial is the Wilde Wege-Wild Ways project, which suggests not to construct a new pedestrian platform but to knit together ones rediscovered in the abandoned tram stations and train lines. Acropolis Place defines a route to the building, a connection with Dimitris Pikionis's existing path system, a mood of walking, platforms for the exhibition, a place.

7 Peter and Alison Smithson, *The Charged Void: Architecture*, 161.
8 Peter and Alison Smithson, *The Charged Void: Architecture*, 502

During the 1990s, the Smithsons concentrated their work on the topic of
"the space between." These spaces are often considered leftover spaces—a result
of the more considered placement of the built structure. These spaces are under-
considered in terms of their use and occupation, and as a result they cannot
really be considered empty in the positive and generative sense that Peter
describes. With their interventions at the Tecta Factory, Peter and Alison worked
in these not-yet-empty territories. By considering, inhabiting, and using these
spaces with only extreme subtlety, they made them empty with all the beauty
and ambiguity that the word implies. About these projects Peter wrote this
passage:

*Where there is a sandy beach with rocks standing-up from it, as the tide recedes
small pools are left at certain places where the rocks cluster.*
*It is, as this, that our urbanism acts; the formation of the buildings carry with it an
empooling of the space-between. And as with the rock-pools what is within that
space-between seems extraordinarily vivid.*
*The empooling has not been wholly consciously sought, it is in large part sponta-
neous, consequent to observation of, and invention from, the land-forms, the
boundaries, and the direction of the sun's travel over the working day.*[9]

On our final day with Peter, after all the discussions, his *In Response to the Glut*
lecture, and visits to the well-known Phoenix architectural sites—Taliesen,
Cosanti, etc.—we stopped to see Frank Lloyd Wright's little gem, the Boomer
House. The current owner, Lucille Kintor, has lived in and with this house since
shortly after it was constructed in 1953. Built on the edge of the Biltmore Resort
and the rocky desert, this small house was designed as a modest getaway from
the constraints of the leisure class. Barely 800 square feet, the original house
took advantage of the barren site, amazing views, and intense desert light. In the
early photos, the sharp angles of the house that stretch in several directions

9 Peter Smithson, "Empooling," in Catherine
Spellman, ed., *Re-Envisioning
Landscape/Architecture* (Barcelona: Actar, 2003),
73.

made the house look like a complicated kite floating just above the ground.
From these photos it is hard to imagine the house lived in. Now it is difficult to
photograph the house from the same vantage point, as the site has very much
been transformed. Through nurture and careful maintenance, Lucille has pulled it
down onto the ground—or rather has helped the ground grow up to meet it. Every
seedling that arrived with the wind and took hold on the site was encouraged to
grow. Today the house is a tree in the jungle that grows around it. In a similar
way, the interior of the house has been taken over by Lucille's life. With an astute
understanding of what it means to live in the desert and with respect and
sensitivity toward Wright's ideas, Lucille inhabits this house. Its strange spaces,
complex structure, and jarring angles feel ordinary with this particular patina of
time. Full of stuff, this house is also empty, for every object that has come to rest
plays a part in constructing the space of the house. On touring the home, Peter
said "Lucille made this house one of Wright's finest works."[10]

Peter's questions about glut and emptiness are essentially Puritan: *Is it right
to have so much? Can we get the quality out of almost nothing? Is experiencing
an empty space a luxury?* To arrive at these questions, one must have gone
through a process of aging, which has a deeper impact on one's work. Otherwise
the response to such questions might be dogmatic or offer reduction as a
simple solution.

From the start, Le Corbusier talked and wrote about pure geometric shapes
under the sun. The concrete shuttering devices in the Villa Shodhan of 1952, the
Millowners Building of 1954, or the Carpenter Centre of 1961–64 indicate in the
most direct way that he was able to express this idea on a new level. The obvious
functional description was not forgotten, yet now he was able to make the light
speak. The invention of the light-controlling concrete skin allowed him to play.
This volume and its material reveal Le Corbusier's history of discoveries with

10 Peter Smithson, conversation with authors,
November, 2001.

light, allowing his projects to speak on another level. Similarly, in their early Brutalist buildings, Alison and Peter Smithson try to make the brick express brickness and the metal express metalness—ideas about the building. Now Peter is talking about glut. We could accept it as a response to consumer society, but we could also say that the emptying of the building, not the building itself, makes room for humanity. Now he is not using material for self-expression, but for preparing the human expression, trying to get as close as possible to life.

In *The Charged Void: Architecture*, Alison and Peter Smithson describe what has been consistent in their work from the beginning:

Observing, studying, and working with the city and metropolis as fabrics. The meaning of the idea of the street and the organization of buildings through their internal streets. Something—a courtyard, a square, a path or a garden—which cannot be altered without difficulties by future activities. The organization of building fabrics by means which are experienced beyond the visual. [11]

The most important consistency in the work of Alison and Peter Smithson, however, is their questioning of what is going on and their willingness to take a position. In the end, this has caused earthquakes from which we still feel the tremors.

11 Peter and Alison Smithson, *The Charged Void: Architecture*, 162.